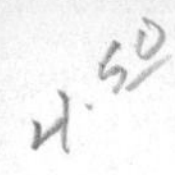

The Story of the Torpedo Bomber

By

Peter C. Smith

ALMARK PUBLISHING CO. LTD. LONDON

First published 1974.

ISBN 0 85524 192 6 (paper cover edition)
ISBN 0 85524 193 4 (hard cover edition)

Printed in Great Britain by
Davenport Askew & Co. Ltd.,
24 Wates Way, Mitcham, Surrey.
for the publishers, Almark Publishing Co. Ltd.
49 Malden Way, New Malden, Surrey KT3 6EA, England.

For
Franz Selinger and Hanfried Schliephake
With thanks and admiration.

The author and publisher wish to thank the following organizations and individuals for their kindness in allowing them to reproduce the photographs featured in this book: Aeronautica Italiana; Archiv Schliephake; Crown Copyright Office; French Navy; Imperial War Museum; Japanese Navy; Real Photos: Franz Selinger; Ufficio Storico; United States Navy

By the same author:

Destroyer Leader
Task Force 57
Pedestal
Stuka at War
Hard Lying
British Battle Cruisers
War in the Aegean (with Edwin Walker)
Heritage of the Sea
Destroyer Action (An anthology — as Editor)
Battles of the Malta Striking Forces (with Edwin Walker)
Royal Navy Ships Badges

CONTENTS

1: Early Developments 7

2: The Inter-War Years 16

3: The Early War Years 23

4: Triumph in Battle 36

5: Decline and Abandonment 63

Introduction

The story of the torpedo bomber has for long needed recording. This book may be looked upon as a pictorial outline of an involved story but one which presents the basic facts and details many of the great actions, supplemented by a comprehensive series of photographs.

The torpedo bomber had a long and slow development from before the Great War and reached maturity in the brief years 1940 to 1942, when spectacular achievements brought it to the forefront of naval warfare. The development of effective anti-aircraft defence and the declining number of suitable targets eventually caused its eclipse during the latter war years. Its final development took place in the early 1950's.

It is now only the anti-submarine torpedo that is taken to sea in aircraft, a development outside the scope of this book but one which has assured the use of the aerial torpedo in a new form at sea for many decades.

Needingworth, Cambs. November 1973.

1: Early Developments

Italy

The Italians were among the first pioneers in the field of torpedoes in the late 19th. century and later were also prominent in the art of torpedo dropping from aircraft. In 1912, a lawyer named Pateras Pescara approached the Italian Ministry of Marine with the proposal that launching torpedoes from an aeroplane was a practical proposition. In the restricted waters of the Mediterranean such an idea showed high promise for future operations against shipping. The Italian navy ordered Lieutenant Allessandro Guidoni to assist in the design and testing of the devices.

Initial tests were carried out by Guidoni flying a Farman biplane on floats equipped with Forlinini vanes. Take-offs and landings were carried out in Venice harbour. As no available Italian aircraft were suitable for carrying a torpedo payload, reaction from designers and pilots was far from enthusiastic. Therefore, Guidoni, working closely with Pescara, designed his own aircraft especially for the task. This aircraft, the Pateras Pescara, had a wingspan of 71 feet 6 inches and was a monoplane, again on two floats equipped with hydro-vanes. It was powered by a Gnome 18-cylinder rotary engine of 160 horse power. This aircraft was

Left: A mass crossing of the Atlantic by Italian Idrovolante S.55 torpedo bombers in 1933 brought home to the world at large, the potential threat to shipping from the torpedo bomber. Right: In 1912, Lieutenant Guidoni, of the Italian navy, flew a Farman biplane to conduct the first torpedo dropping experiments.

Left: The Caproni 33 was used as a torpedo bomber by the Italians in World War I. Below: The Pateras Pescara monoplane, first flown by Guidoni in 1914, was the first aircraft to be designed as a torpedo bomber. Below right: The Short 184 was the first British torpedo bomber. It first came into service in 1915, when it was used against Turkish shipping during the Gallipoli campaign.

completed in 1914 and Guidoni flew it on its maiden flight. During the tests which followed a torpedo of about 820 lbs. was successfully launched.

When World War I broke out in August 1914, Italy was initially neutral, and Guidoni using the Italian hydroplane carrying ship *Elba,* moored in Venice harbour, continued with his experiments. Soon, however, the involvement of Italy in the war forced the *Elba* to leave for Taranto. As a result of this, the Pescara monoplane was left to rot away in a corner of the Navy Arsenal at Venice, and plans for torpedo launching aircraft were abandoned for a time.

After Italy entered the war on the Allied side in 1915, her major opponent was Austro-Hungary. The Italians revived the development of the torpedo bomber in order to attack the Austro-Hungarian fleet across the Adriatic Sea. Effective launchings were carried out during August 1917 from the Caproni Ca.33, illustrated here, and the Ca.34 and these were followed by the tri-motor Caproni Ca.46 and Ca.47. On September 20th, 1917, an ammunition base at Pola was attacked by an Italian torpedo bomber piloted by Ridolfi with Pacchiarotti as his navigator. In 1918, Gabriele D'Annunzio formed the first torpedo bomber unit and thus the famed *Aerosilurante* had its beginnings.

Great Britain

The Royal Navy was not backward in developing the torpedo bomber. Lieutenant A.M. Longmore, later to become Air Chief Marshal Sir Arthur Longmore, made a successful torpedo drop at Calshot on 28th. July, 1914 in a 160 horse power Gnome-powered Short seaplane during experiments with the 14-inch, 850 lb. Whitehead torpedo. A leading British

advocate of the torpedo bomber was Commodore Murry F. Sueter, and after the outbreak of World War I, he pressed his point with the firm of Short Brothers at Rochester in Kent.

As a result of the collaboration between Sueter and Short Brothers the famous Short 184 seaplane was developed. This was a two-seater biplane powered by a 225 horse power Sunbeam engine. It had a wingspan of 63 feet, $6\frac{1}{4}$ inches, an overall length of 40 feet $7\frac{1}{2}$ inches and a height of 13 feet 6 inches. Maximum speed was $88\frac{1}{2}$ m.p.h. at 2,000 feet and it could carry a single 14-inch torpedo. It was to be known as the '225' after its engine power, in service.

The Royal Navy made its first successful torpedo bombing attacks during the Dardenelles campaign in 1915. The first deliveries of the Short 184 were made to the Royal Naval Air Service at Mudros in June 1915. They began operations from the seaplane carrier *Ben my Chree.* On August 12th., Flight-Commander C.H.K. Edmonds flying one of these aircraft from the Gulf of Xeros was over the Sea of Marmara when he sighted a large steamer. He glided down to within 300 yards range before releasing his torpedo which struck the vessel abreast the mainmast. He could not confirm that the ship was sunk but there was no doubt at all when, on the 17th. August, he made an attack on a convoy of three vessels heading for Ak Bashi Liman. One steamer was hit and set on fire, and although towed to Constantinople it was burnt out as a total loss. Flight Lieutenant G.B. Dacre had also scored a similar success with the '225' sinking a tug. He made his attack while taxiing across the water after engine failure and subsequently made his escape under fire from Turkish coastal batteries.

Germany

The Imperial German navy sponsored the design of a torpedo bomber on floats early in the war, but there were few actual operations by torpedo carrying aircraft on the German side. In the main these aircraft were used for scouting and reconnaissance duties in addition to orthodox bombing sorties.

In Imperial Germany, the Albatros B.II was one of the many types of aircraft modified to carry torpedoes.

The torpedo-carrying gear of an almost completed Gotha WD.11 is tested with a practice torpedo.

The Imperial German Navy ordered a total of twenty-two aircraft from the Hansa Brandenburg Flugzeug Werke at Brandenburg to the designs of Ernst Heinkel. From the Gothaer Waggonfabrik (Railcar Factory) the German Navy ordered three types between 1916 and 1918. The first of these was the Type WD11. It was a three-seater, twin-engined biplane on floats, which had a span of 73 feet and a length of 44 feet. Powered by two Mercedes 160 horse power engines driving pusher airscrews it had a maximum speed of 75 m.p.h. and a total of seventeen were built.

The Albatros Flugzeugwerke also designed torpedo carrying aircraft but did not ultimately receive orders for serial production. The design was the Type W.3 with two Mercedes 160 horse power engines, and it was delivered in July 1916 as Navy number 527. Also produced was the W.5 with two Benz 150 horse power engines, four of which, numbers 846 to 849, were built. They had a span of 74 feet, a length of 42 feet and had a maximum speed of 82 m.p.h.

Although actions by German torpedo bombers were few, one significant event took place

Lett: A total of 22 Hansa Brandenburg torpedo reconnaissance floatplanes, such as the one pictured here, were ordered by the Imperial German Navy.

in September 1916. Lieutenant Fritz W. Hammer was one of the pilots operational with a German Seeflieger Abteilung based at Angern See on the Gulf of Riga, in the Baltic. Their flying activities were concentrated mainly on reconnaissance and fighting Russian aircraft, but plans were discussed to make the best use of the four torpedo carrying aircraft of the unit.

In a combined operation with a naval force, the Russian battleship *Slava* and destroyer escorts, were lured into leaving their secure anchorage at Moon Sound on September 12th., 1916. At 5.45 p.m. the four German torpedo aircraft, led by a single engined floatplane with the squadron commander, took off from Angern See station. They were accompanied by ordinary bombers, which were to bomb the Russian warships and thus distract their attention while the torpedo bombers attacked at sea level. This was probably the first practical demonstration by an air force of the synchronised attack.

Twenty nautical miles north of Domesnes the *Slava* and five destroyers were sighted and were attacked by the bombers. The torpedo bombers turned on a parallel course to the warships to work their way into the best position to make a stern attack. At a distance of 1600 yards the torpedo bombers turned 90 degrees and released their missiles broadside to the battleship. By this time, one of the torpedo aircraft had dropped out of the attack due to engine failure. The remaining three attacked at intervals of about four seconds. The first torpedo failed to run, due to damage caused by hitting part of the aircraft when released. The second ran short before diving to the bottom of the sea. The third ran straight and true, but one of the destroyers crossed the track before it reached the *Slava* but was not sent to the bottom. Although anti-aircraft fire was intense, none of the German aircraft were damaged.

The Flugzeugbau Fridrichshafen company was another well known producer of German single engined seaplanes. They also, however, produced a twin-engined floatplane, the FF 41A, nine of which entered service during World War I. With a span of 71 feet 6 inches and a length of 44 feet 6 inches, it was powered by two Benz 150 horse power engines giving a maximum speed of 78 m.p.h. and a range of 350 miles.

The second major type produced by Gotha was the WD 14. A total of seventy of this very successful aircraft were delivered to the German Navy. Generally similar to the WD 11 they

Above left: An Albatros W8. Above right: Early trials of torpedo carrying were made with the L.D.V. G.4. Below: A Gotha WD.11 afloat.

Below left: A Gotha WD 14 stands outside a hangar. Below right: The German seaplane station at Norderney in 1917.

Above: During World War I, nine FF 41 A twin engined floatplanes were built by the Flugzeugbau Frildrichshafen company. Below: A WD.11 is towed at speed behind a German destroyer in an experiment to see if floatplanes could be launched by this method. Below right: The Gotha WD.20 was developed from the WD.11 and the WD.14.

were fitted with two Benz 200 horse power engines driving tractor airscrews. Span was 81 feet 3 inches and length was 47 feet 1 inch with a maximum speed of 80 m.p.h.

The final development of the Gotha series was the WD22 a four-engined biplane with the engines in tandem driving tractor and pusher airscrews. The front engines were Mercedes D III 160 horse power and the rear were Mercedes D.I. 100 horse power types. Speed was 81 m.p.h. and range was 465 miles. Only two were built.

Austro Hungary

One Gotha aircraft of the WD series number 1661 was delivered to the Austro-Hungarian Navy Aviation on 4th. July, 1918 but was not used operationally. Also delivered was an improved Hansa Brandenburg GW known as the GWd. It was built as a single prototype with the number 701. It had a span of 79 feet, a length of 51 feet and was powered by two Benz engines each of 220 horse power which gave a speed of 80 m.p.h. This aircraft was delivered to Germany's ally on 23rd. November 1917 after a ferry flight from Flensburg on the Baltic to Pola with various stops for fuelling.

Both these aircraft were to be fully tested in the Adriatic, but were not finally used much as torpedo bombers. The Austro-Hungarian navy was against the whole concept of the torpedo bomber because it was widely believed that the aerial torpedo would dive too steeply on entering the water and stick in the mud. This applied especially, it was thought, to the shallow waters of the Adriatic. Torpedo bomber attacks were practical, it was assumed, only against moored ships.

2: The Inter-War Years

Although both Japan and the United States of America entered World War I on the Allied side, they were both too far from the European battlefields to exert much influence on aerial matters. But both had shown interest in the torpedo bomber concept and, although they lacked war experience, both were to advance this concept more than other nations between the wars.

Japan

Japan set up the Naval Aeronautical Research Committee in June 1912, but little progress had been made by the end of the war. In 1922, two Blackburn Mk-2 Swifts were sent to Japan from Britain and based at Kasumigaura Naval Air Station forty miles to the north of Tokyo. Lieutenant Commander H.G. Brackley was sent to train Japanese pilots in torpedo dropping and his success was to become only too evident less than twenty years later! The first Japanese carrier, the *Honsho,* was ready for trials at sea during this period. The Swift had a span of 48 feet 6 inches, a length of 36 feet and a height of 13 feet 3 inches. Fitted with a Packard engine, the maximum speed was 123 m.p.h. and the range was 300 miles.

The Mitsubishi B1M1 Type 13 carrier born attack bomber was the next development in

A Japanese torpedo bomber of the 1920's.

Japan, but in 1927 the Imperial Navy decided upon its replacement. In a competition, a Mitsubishi sponsored Blackburn design, the Ka-3 two-seater biplane, was declared the winner. This was first flown on 28th. December, 1929 and was shipped to Japan from Britain early the following year. As the Type 89 a total of 205 B2M's served aboard the carriers *Ryujo, Akagi* and *Kaga* between 1933 and 1937.

United States

In the United States, Admiral Bradley A. Fiske had proposed the adoption of the torpedo bomber type before 1914. Glenn Curtiss were the firm selected to build the first Navy aircraft, the A-1 Triad, which was first flown on 1st. July, 1911. In 1913, the base at Annapolis was set up and, on 1st. July, 1915, the office of Naval Aeronautics was established. Trials were carried out with torpedo bombers on 11th. August, 1917 but were failures.

After the Great War, Curtiss R-6L's were modified to carry the naval torpedo. The aircraft was a two seater with a 400 horse power Liberty-V12 engine. It had a span of 57 feet 1¼ inches, a length of 33 feet 6 inches and a height of 14 feet. Maximum speed was 100 m.p.h. and range was 565 miles. Other types were developed in a determined effort to produce a torpedo bomber for the Navy in the twenties and common features were in line, water cooled engines, biplane construction and interchangeable wheel or float chassis.

Between October 1922 and March 1923 three new American types and three Fokker Ft-1 twin-float monoplanes were tested at Anacosta. The aircraft selected from these tests was the Douglas DT.1. This was the first military aircraft produced by the Douglas Aircraft Corporation. With a span of 50 feet, a length of 37 feet 7½ inches and a height of 15 feet 1 inch, the DT.1 had a range of 274 miles and a maximum speed of 99 m.p.h. at sea level. It could carry a 1,835 pound torpedo.

Delivered in 1921, and exhaustively tested, the DT-1 was so successful that 38 improved versions, the DT-2, were ordered and delivered in 1922 to the San Diego Naval Air Station, joining VT-2. By 1925 it had replaced the R.-6L in Navy service. DT-2's were also used in test launchings from the first U.S. Navy carrier, the *Langley* in 1925.

They in turn were to be replaced later by the Curtiss CS-1 of 1923, which was the first torpedo bomber, as such, produced by this company. Six joined VT-1 in April 1924. On 12th. October, 1925 the Martin T3M was contracted for. With steel tube fuselage this two seater was powered by a 770 horse power Packard engine and had a span of 56 feet, and length of 41 feet 4 inches. Maximum speed was 109 m.p.h. In September 1926, they began to enter service with VT-1 aboard the *Lexington.*

Still dissatisfied, the Navy called for another torpedo bomber type and this resulted in the Douglas T2D. This two-seater biplane was powered by two Wright R-1750 engines developing 525 horse power. Wingspan was 57 feet, length 45 feet and maximum speed was 124 m.p.h. at sea level. It could carry a 1,618 lb. torpedo for a range of 422 miles. The first T20-1 joined the *Langley* with VT-2 on 25th. May, 1927 and became the first two-engined aircraft to be launched from a carrier. The final American torpedo bomber of this period was the Martin BM which was designed for the dual role of dive and torpedo bombing. Like most such compromises it could do only one job really well, and was used for dive bombing until 1937.

Above: The Italian Caproni Ca.44 made its first appearance in August 1917. Left: The torpedo mounting on a CA.44.

Italy

As the originators of the torpedo bomber, the Italians had re-vitalised their earlier interest once the success of the British and German designs had become apparent during World War I. Both nations' designs had similar faults in that they were not powerful enough to lift heavy torpedoes without cutting down the weight of the warhead. Thus, in theory anyway, the weapon they delivered to the target was less effective than a standard bomb. Because of this the Royal Air Force and the Luftwaffe both concentrated on developing aircraft for conventional bombing throughout the 1930's. The Italians set about producing an aircraft capable of carrying a heavier torpedo. The Caproni Ca-44, which appeared in August 1917, formed the basis from which the later Ca.46 and Ca.47 were developed.

Great Britain

The R.N.A.S. had pressed on with successful designs and, by 1918, was far ahead of the rest of the world in performance and experience. Again Sueter was the driving force and, in 1916, he got together with the Sopwith Aviation Company at Kingston-upon-Thames, already famed for their scout and fighter aircraft. The result was the famous T1, the Cuckoo.

The Cuckoo was a single-seater biplane powered by a single 200 horse power Sunbeam Arab engine which gave it a speed of 103 m.p.h. at 2,000 feet. The wingspan was 46 feet 9 inches, and the length was 28 feet 6 inches. It carried a Mk-IX 18-inch torpedo externally. The Cuckoo first entered service in July 1918, and ninety had been delivered by the time of the Armistice. Production continued post war and Cuckoos went to sea aboard the *Eagle* in October 1918. The last were not finally phased out of service until 1923 by which time, they had served also aboard the carrier *Argus*.

It was found that the 1,086 pound torpedo was too light to inflict serious damage on ships and by the autumn of 1917 the Admiralty was seeking an aircraft capable of carrying the Mk-VIII 1,423 pound torpedo which had a fifty percent larger warhead. Two aircraft, the Blackburd and the Sirl were produced to meet this specification and after trials on the Humber in May 1918, the Blackburd was finally selected. The wingspan was 52 feet 5 inches, and the length 34 feet 10 inches. The single engine enabled the Blackburd to carry the heavier weapon at a speed of 90.5 m.p.h. Meanwhile, the Blackburn company had developed the T1 Swift as a private venture in 1919. The T1 Swift underwent trials at Gosport followed by deck trials aboard the *Argus* when it was piloted by Gerald Boyce. Successful results led to deliveries to the U.S.A., Japan, Spain and Brazil.

An improved version of the Swift was the T2 Dart. A single seater powered by a 450 horse power Napier Lion engine, it had a wingspan of 45 feet 6 inches, a length of 35 feet 6 inches and maximum speed of 110 m.p.h. at sea level. Following trials aboard *Argus* in 1921, the Dart was adopted as the standard torpedo bomber. 117 were built, serving at sea aboard the

Below left: The Sopwith Cuckoo, pictured here launching a torpedo, was in service with the Royal Navy from 1918 to 1923. Below right: A Blackburn T2 Dart drops a torpedo.

Eagle and *Furious*. The potential of the torpedo bomber was emphasised when, during combined fleet exercises off the Isle of Wight on 9th. September, 1930, an attack by fifteen Darts from Lee-on-Solent scored eight hits on Britain's latest battleships, the *Nelson* and *Rodney*.

The R.N.A.S. had become part of the R.A.F. in 1918 and the R.A.F. operated all aircraft from the fleet's carriers. In consequence, the development of naval aircraft underwent a dramatic decline. It was regarded as a backwater by R.A.F. pilots and was voted very limited funds. As a result, during the late 1920's and the 1930's the Royal Navy's once commanding lead in the field of naval aviation was thrown away.

Developed from the Dart was the Blackburn Velos which was a two seater. The Velos was powered by a 450 horse power Napier Lion V engine and was developed as a floatplane, a batch of sixteen were sold to the Greek Navy for coastal defence requirements after being tested by Guidoni himself and others in October 1925.

Blackburn's successful association with torpedo bombers continued in the late 1920's through the ugly Blackburn Blackburn to the elegant Ripon which was the Dart's replacement in Naval service. The Blackburn Ripon was a two-seater biplane, powered by a 750 horse power Napier Lion XIA engine. Wingspan was 44 feet 10 inches and length was 36 feet, 9 inches. With a maximum speed of 126 m.p.h. at sea level and twice the range of the Dart, the Ripon was a very popular aircraft and first entered service in August 1929. Only 92 were built in all between 1928 and December 1933, which gives some idea of the lack of effort devoted to the Fleet Air Arm.

The Blackburn Velos torpedo bomber was developed from the Blackburn Dart.

Above left: A Blackburn Ripon airborne with a torpedo. Above right: The same Ripon on the ground. Below left: A "Stringbag" Fairey Swordfish. Below right: A formation of Blackburn Baffins photographed in 1937.

Another torpedo bomber with a Blackburn pedigree was the Baffin which was first flown by Flight Lieutenant A.M. Blake in June 1933. It was a two-seater biplane, powered by a single Bristol Pegasus 565 horse power engine, giving a speed of 136 m.p.h.

At the outbreak of World War II, the Royal Navy's front line torpedo bomber was the biplane Fairey Swordfish. Ending Blackburn's long run of torpedo bombers for a short period, the Swordfish replaced the Blackburn Shark when it entered squadron service in 1938. The Swordfish was obsolete before the war began. Due to the dedication and fearlessness of the young Fleet Air Arm crews, the old 'Stringbag' remained in service and covered itself in glory, but how much more could have been achieved with modern aircraft.

The three-seater Swordfish was powered by a 690 horse power Bristol Pegasus II engine. Wingspan was 45 feet 6 inches, length 36 feet 4 inches and maximum speed was 139 m.p.h. at 4,750 feet. Later versions were powered by a 750 horse power Pegasus XXX engine. First flown on 17th. April, 1934, the Swordfish was still serving operationally more than ten years later and its exploits were legendary. At the outbreak of the war Swordfish were embarked in the *Ark Royal, Courageous, Eagle, Glorious* and *Furious.*

While Great Britain was diligently plodding on with biplane after biplane, gaining 20 m.p.h. or so with each new design, other nations were taking larger strides. The seaplane concept however, died hard, even in Italy. A massed crossing of the Atlantic by Idrovolante S.55's in 1933 was given great publicity and the menace to ships from aerial torpedos carried at such ranges was obvious (see frontispiece).

A Fairey Swordfish Mark I, photographed in 1935.

Germany

When Germany began to re-arm in the 1930's it might have been expected that, after the successes of World War I, the development of the torpedo bomber would have been given some priority. But Goering, like his counterparts in the R.A.F. was not interested in maritime affairs. As a result development rested solely upon the Navy and with limited funds it lagged. Again seaplanes were the most favoured types. Even when the first carrier, the *Graf Zeppelin,* was laid down, her main offensive aircraft were to be Stuka dive-bombers.

Below left: Heinkel He.114 aircrew and ground staff stage a scramble at a German floatplane base. Below right: A rare photograph of a Heinkel He.59 carrying a torpedo.

3: The Early War Years

Italy

The Italian airforce experimented with radical approaches. The original role of the Savoia Marchetti SM.79-1 was as an altitude bomber in the Spanish Civil War. After repeated attempts at mass bombing attacks against the British Mediterranean Fleet in July and August of 1940, it quickly became evident that altitude bombing against warships with the bombs and instruments of the day was useless.

The result was the conversion to the torpedo bombing role of the SM.79-11, powered by three 1,000 horse power Piaggip P.XI engines, although the idea had been fostered for many years prior to the war. The SM-79 was to be one of the most outstanding of the land based torpedo types and its name, the Sparrow, became as famous in Italy as the Spitfire was in Britain. Trials were held at Gorizia in 1937 with the standard 17.7 inch naval torpedo, fitted with a 375 pound warhead. Using a special rack offset from the centre line of the plane and a newly developed launching sight, this torpedo quickly proved itself. Attempts made later to fit the SM.79 with two such mountings were ultimately successful although they affected the aircraft's performance. The Italians established a torpedo bomber training school at Grosseto on Italy's west coast and, after many early conventional bombing attacks had failed against British warships, more and more squadrons were switched over to this type of warfare.

The Fiat BR.20.-Bis was another standard medium bomber which underwent a similar adaptation to enable it to play a more prominent part in the air-sea war which was so dominant in the Mediterranean theatre.

The Italians had devoted considerable resources towards the maritime aspect of their air force, no doubt with the view that any war with Britain and France would be decided ultimately at sea due to Italy's exposed position in the Mediterranean.

The SM.84 was adapted to carry a special device for use against warships and convoys known as the *Motobomba.* Colonel Lionello Leone who commanded 132 *Stormo* based at Bari had described to the author the function of these weapons which were in effect circling mines or torpedoes. Each SM.84 could carry two of these weapons which had a weight of 400-kg. Leone described them as *naval* weapons which were dropped perpendicularly by parachute. On impact with the sea the parachute automatically released itself. A gyroscopically-controlled motor then started and at three-metres depth a syphon of mercury started the motor and fins which would drive the *motobomba* forward with a spinning motion, without leaving any tell-tale wake behind it. They were self-destructive and had a maximum time allowance of twelve hours.

The Italian *Aerosilurante* units, although merely a small fraction of the total Italian air effort, made their mark on the air-sea battles taking place in the Mediterranean. Among these handful of pilots, several soon became famous for their skill and accuracy. They

Above and below: Savoia Marchetti SM.79's. The bottom photograph, taken during the Spanish Civil War, shows the SM.79 in its original role as an altitude bomber.

included such pilots as Deodato, Erasi, Mauri, Robone, Sabatini and, the most famous Italian torpedo bomber ace of them all, Carlo Emmanuele Buscaglia.

An early attack on Alexandria harbour on the 15th. August, 1940, failed to materialize; however, the SM.79's were very active in daring twilight attacks at dusk and dawn on ships of the Mediterranean Fleet. No less than three cruisers fell to their torpedo attacks in the eastern Mediterranean during a two-month period. On the night of 17th. September, a British naval squadron was caught returning from a bombardment of Bardia and an attack in brilliant moonlight by the SM.79's resulted in a hit on the heavy cruiser *Kent*. This was a particularly valuable result for the Italians because the *Kent,* which had 8-inch guns had only recently joined Admiral Cunningham's fleet. Until the arrival of the *Kent,* together with the *York,* the British cruiser had been outgunned by the Italian ships. By torpedoing the *Kent,* the Italians partially maintained their advantage.

This initial success was repeated when the *Aerosilurante* made another attack on the fleet as it was returning to Alexandria after a sortie on the 14th. October. The fleet was attacked again at dusk and one SM.79 hit the cruiser *Liverpool* in the bows. The explosion ignited a petrol tank which in turn detonated her forward magazine. The whole of the *Liverpool's*

Above: A Fiat BR.20Bis. Below: A Savoia Marchetti SM.84.

bows before the bridge were wrecked and hung down into the water. Taken in tow by the *Orion* and destroyers, the crippled cruiser struggled back to Alexandria, the damaged bow dropping off on the way in.

Yet a third success took place on 3rd. December, 1940, when the cruiser *Glasgow,* newly arrived to replace the *Liverpool,* was caught by two SM.79's while at anchor in Suda Bay, Crete. The British warships were taken completely by surprise and no fire was opened against them. Consequently, both aircraft were able to place their torpedos firmly into the *Glasgow* at 3,000 yards range. Very severely damaged the *Glasgow* was the third cruiser to limp back through the Suez Canal on a forlorn journey to the repair yards of Britain or America.

All these attacks were the work of one squadron, Buscaglia's 278 Squadriglia, operating in two sections based respectively at El Adem in Libya and at Rhodes in the Aegean. On 27th. December, a second unit, 279 Squadriglia, finished its training at Gorizia and moved to the operational base in Sicily for operations against British convoys attempting to force the straits and relieve Malta. These two were joined by yet a third, 281 Squadriglia, based on Rhodes, in March 1941.

France

The French navy was not prominent at any time in the field of torpedo bombing, and only a single carrier was operational pre-war. Due to this restriction they tended to develop the old concept of the floatplane, as indeed had Britain to a small extent and Germany almost exclusively. The rapid defeat of France resulted in no activity in their limited torpedo bomber force against the Axis. Two of France's most modern torpedo bombers in service prior to June 1940 were the Latecoere Late 290 and the Latecoere Late 298 01.

Left: A Latecoere Late 298. Below: A Latecoere Late 290.

Above: A He.115 launches a practice torpedo at a target ship in the Baltic. Inset: A Heinkel He.115 being loaded with a torpedo.

Germany

In Germany limited progress had been made in World War I with floatplanes. The German Navy had a few torpedo bombers on its strength, the He.115 replacing the He.59 in the torpedo bomber and general-purpose role in 1938. This twin-engined plane was an advanced design for its time and its excellent handling qualities ensured that it remained in front-line service throughout the war. The Arado Ar.95, a single-engined floatplane powered by a 880 horse power BMW-132-DC engine was designed for use as a catapault aircraft for German heavy ships. It could also carry the standard torpedo when required. Blohm and Voss were famed for their long-range scouting aircraft during the Second World War and the twin-engined BV-140 torpedo aircraft was another of their wartime products.

The main striking force of the German Navy's torpedo bombers were the He.115's. Good though these aircraft were, only a few were actually ready for operations on 3rd. September, 1939, one *Staffel* only (nine aircraft) serving with the *Seeflieger* (Coastal) forces. They were used for minelaying as much as for torpedo operations.

Above left: An Arado Ar.95 carrying a torpedo. Above right: A Blohm and Voss BV.140 torpedo bomber.

This chronic shortage of torpedo aircraft can be laid partly at the door of Goering who had no understanding and little interest in maritime warfare. But an equally important factor was that between 1933 and 1940 the German Navy failed to recreate the success of its World War 1 aircraft and operations. In 1933, the Navy purchased the Horten naval torpedo patents from Norway as a first step and this was followed in 1938 by the obtaining of similar patents from Italy for the Whitehead-Fiume torpedo. Despite this, subsequent development was leisurely. During extensive torpedo dropping trials, carried out in 1939, both the He.59 and the He.115 were used and the failure rate of the torpedoes was a staggering 49 percent. This was due to aerodynamic difficulties in launching from aircraft, depth control problems and fusing failures.

So it was that the limited He.115 force operated by the Navy did not have a high success rate during the opening years of the war. Only two dozen floatplanes were engaged in limited torpedo attacks on British convoys off the coast of Scotland and in the Western Approaches. The Luftwaffe ignored the torpedo bomber carrying out its attacks with Junkers 87 dive-bombers in coastal waters. These had great success in the Channel in the summer of 1940 and many victories in the Mediterranean during 1941/42, medium bombers were also used from time to time.

Therefore few sinkings were recorded by German aerial torpedoes during this period, and scarcity of aircraft was worsened by an equal shortage of torpedoes. One lone victory was obtained on the 23rd. August, 1940 when convoy OA.203 was attacked in the Moray Firth and two ships were sunk and another damaged.

Japan

In Japan, the torpedo bomber had gone ahead in leaps and bounds, both as a carrier-born and as a land-based aircraft. In 1932 the 7-Shi plan initiated a whole new series of all types. The results of this were disappointing but the 8-Shi plan of 1934 brought much better results.

The first step was the Yokosuka B4Y 'Jean' which was a single-engined three-seater carrier-born biplane. Wing span was 49 feet 2½ inches, length 33 feet, 3½ inches and height was 14 feet 3½ inches. The Jean could carry a 1,764 pound torpedo into action at 173 m.p.h. and had a range of 978 miles. When Japan ultimately entered the war in December 1941, this aircraft was widely believed to be the standard equipment of the Japanese Navy.

Also produced under the 8-Shi plan of 1934 was the Mitsubishi G3M2 'Nell'. This was a great advance in torpedo bomber design. Designated the Type-96 attack bomber, it was originated by Admiral Yamamoto while he was serving as chief of the Technical Division of the Naval Bureau of Aeronautics. This twin-engined sleek monoplane had a five-man crew and could carry a 1,764 pound torpedo into attacks at a speed of 258 m.p.h. It was land based and had the outstanding range of 3,871 miles. Wingspan was 82 feet, length 54 feet and height 12 feet 11 inches.

The most advanced carrier-born torpedo bomber in the world in 1940 was the Imperial Japanese Navy's Nakajima B5N2, Type-97 attack plane, designated by Allied forces, the 'Kate'. Produced under the 10-Shi programme of 1936 it first went into production in November 1937, (Model 11). By December 1939, the Type-12, a much improved version, was entering service. A single-engined, three seater monoplane,it was the first plane thrown into action at Pearl Harbor. Carrying the standard torpedo, the Kate had a top speed of 235 m.p.h. at 11,800 feet and a maximum range of 1,237 miles. Wing span was 50 feet 11 inches, length 33 feet 9½ inches and height 12 feet 2 inches.

The Mitsubishi G4M2 Navy Type-1 Land attack plane, the 'Betty' was another land-based torpedo bomber of the Imperial Japanese Navy. Development of this aircraft began in September 1937, under a replacement programme for the Nell. Its outstanding feature was its range of 3,765 miles. In addition, it was the first torpedo bomber to carry its torpedo internally. It had a crew of seven and a top speed of 272 m.p.h. at 15,000 feet. Its chief drawback was its lack of resistance to tracer and it earned for itself the unenviable nickname of the 'Flying Lighter' in battles over the Solomons in 1942/43. Wing span was 82 feet, length 65 feet 8 inches, height 19 feet 8½ inches.

Below: Mitsubishi G3M's were called "Nells" by the Allies. Top right: The Nakajima B5N2, was known as the "Kate". Bottom right: The Mitsubishi G4M2 had the the code name of "Betty".

Above right: A United States Naval Airforce Dauntless "spreads its wings" as it prepares for take-off. These Dauntlesses arrived in Britain in 1942. Above left: A Brewster Bermuda. Left: A Douglas TBD 1 Dauntless in flight.

United States

In the years leading up to the war the United States Navy had developed its own torpedo bombers. However, the Army Air Force had no interest in the torpedo, and therefore land-based long range torpedo aircraft were not a feature of America's developments as they were Japan's. The Navy had pushed ahead with the design of carrier-borne aircraft. With the introduction of the new carrier *Ranger* in 1934, and with more carriers on the stocks, a new range of aircraft was being called for. Prototype torpedo bombers were ordered from the Great Lakes Company and Douglas in June 1934, and from subsequent tests the Douglas TBD-1 was selected. It was the first U.S. Navy carrier-borne monoplane to be put into production. Other features were upward folding wings which were power operated and a semi-retractable under-carriage. Named the Devastator, it was a three-seater aircraft powered by a single 900 horse power Pratt and Whitney engine. The torpedo was carried externally and at a slight forward tilting angle which made this aircraft unmistakeable in flight. Wing span was 50 feet, length 35 feet and height 15 feet 1 inch. Maximum speed was 206 m.p.h. at 8,000 feet. Orders were placed for 130 in 1936 and the first was delivered to VT-3 on 5th. October, 1937. Devastators later joined VT's 2, 5 and 8. The Devastator was still in service at the start of the Pacific war and saw action at the Marshall and Gilbert islands as well as the first great carrier battles.

Great Britain

Monoplanes formed the backbone of the torpedo bomber forces of the United States, Japan, Italy and Germany but the Royal Navy's front line equivalent in 1940 was a biplane. This was the Fairey Albacore, originally designed in 1936 as a replacement for the Swordfish. It featured an enclosed cockpit for the crew, an all-metal fuselage, hydraulic flaps and a remarkably economical engine. Despite these features however, it's other specifications were years behind those of its foreign counterparts.

The Albacore was a single-engined, three-seater biplane. It was powered by a 1,065 horse power Bristol Taurus II engine giving a maximum speed of 161 m.p.h. at 4,000 feet. The externally mounted 1,610 pound torpedo could be carried a maximum range of 930 miles. Wing span was 50 feet, length 39 feet 9½ inches and height was 15 feet 3 inches. In May 1937, one hundred were ordered under an Air Ministry contract. The Fleet Air Arm did not finally revert to full Navy control until later. The result of twenty years of this arrangement was the low quality of the British torpedo bombers.

The first Albacores to go to sea joined the *Formidable* with 826 and 829 Squadrons in November 1940. They were soon in action and in March 1941 scored a hit on the Italian battleship *Vittorio Veneto* while the Swordfish of 815 Squadron hit the heavy cruiser *Pola.* This action led to the Battle of Cape Matapan and a decisive defeat for the Italian Navy at the hands of Admiral Cunningham's battleships. During the preceeding air-sea battles, SM.79's tried to torpedo the *Formidable* but failed. The Albacores, led by Lieutenant

A formation flight of Fleet Air Arm Albacore torpedo bombers start out on an exercise.

A Fairey Albacore in flight.

Commander W.G.H. Saunt, D.S.C., penetrated a heavy barrage to score their hits which left the battleship limping home at reduced speed. The Swordfish left the cruiser disabled and she was later sunk by gunfire.

In March 1942, Albacores from *Victorious* made an attack on the German battleship *Tirpitz* when she sortied out against a Russian convoy off Norway. They failed to hit her, although several torpedoes ran close. Although employed on many fleet and escort carriers from 1941 to 1943 these were the only major attacks carried out by Albacores in the torpedo bomber role. In April 1942, Albacores came close to a duel with a Japanese task force in the Indian Ocean. Admiral Somerville planned to use them in a dusk strike against six big carriers but in view of the reputation of the Japanese fighters it is perhaps fortunate for the Royal Navy that this one battle was not fought.

It is an ironical fact that the old 'Stringbag', which the Albacore was meant to replace outlasted her in service and affection. It was the Swordfish which made the outstanding contributions to the Royal Navy's great victories in 1940/41. During the Norwegian campaign in April and May 1940, the Swordfish had their first chance to show their mettle. On the Italian declaration of war in June, 830 Squadron was established on the island of Malta. When the French fleet followed the orders of the puppet Vichy government, it was

A torpedo is wheeled into position under a Swordfish on the flight deck of a British aircraft-carrier.

Swordfish from the *Ark Royal* which carried out the first torpedo bomber attacks on battleships when they torpedoed the *Dunkerque* at Oran on 6th. July, 1940. They also made the first attack on a battleship at sea in the World War II when they tried to stop the *Strasbourg* escaping to France on the same occasion. Swordfish from the *Eagle* with Admiral Cunningham's fleet off Calabria struck at the Italian fleet on the 9th. July, but failed to score any hits. Swordfish, operating from desert air strips in support of the Army, scored the first of their many successes against the Italians, when on 22nd. August, three Swordfish of 813 Squadron led by Captain Patch, D.S.O., D.S.C., R.M., claimed a submarine, a depot ship and two destroyers in an attack on Bomba harbour in Libya.

Meanwhile the R.A.F. had introduced the Bristol Beaufort as a replacement for the Wildebeest torpedo bomber. Although the Beaufort was intended mainly as a torpedo aircraft of a faster type than hitherto available, early attacks made by these aircraft were made using bombs. The reasons for this state of affairs were that in early 1940 their crews were not fully trained in the new methods of torpedo dropping and, like the Germans, the R.A.F. had a shortage of torpedoes. In fact, when war broke out only two squadrons were equipped for torpedo bombing in the R.A.F., these were 22 and 42 Squadrons and both were equipped with the Wildebeest. Beauforts replaced these in the spring of 1940. The Beaufort was a four seater monoplane powered by two Taurus engines which gave it a top speed of 290 m.p.h.

The switch from the obsolete types to this much more powerful aircraft required new techniques and at Thorny Island and Gosport, Portsmouth these new tactics were given their first tests. Because the Beaufort built up speed very quickly in a dive the old method of diving onto the target from out of effective anti-aircraft range could not be used. Instead, the aircraft had to be at low level throughout the whole approach and it was thus exposed to prolonged fire from its target. Experiments with fitting dive brakes and trials with a new 'flying' torpedo which could be dropped from 1,500 feet were not a success. This later device, known as the 'toraplane' was later to be developed by the Luftwaffe.

On completion of their training, 22 Squadron moved to North Coates airfield in Lincolnshire under the command of Wing Commander F.J.St.G. Braithwaite. They carried out their first torpedo bombing mission on 11th. September, 1940, when five Beauforts led by Flight Lieutenant Dick Beauman struck a convoy between Calais and Ostend. Three torpedoes 'hung up', one exploded prematurely but the final one ran true and destroyed a large merchant ship. All the Beauforts returned safely to base.

Due to the continued shortage of aircraft,the R.A.F. squadrons operated in the North Sea and the Channel in small groups, each aircraft quartering its own sector. These missions were known as 'Rovers' and were to prove an uneconomical method of using such vulnerable aircraft.

In September, six Beauforts of 22 Squadron led by Flight Commander Francis, made a night torpedo attack on shipping assembled at Cherbourg, However, en-route to the attack they ran into heavy cloud which split the formation. The original plan had been for the Beauforts to attack in three waves which would cross the harbour in pairs from the east, north and west and it was hoped that the ships would be silhouetted by fires started by preceeding altitude attacks. Four aircraft made drops, one was shot down over the target zone and another got lost and turned back. Reconnaissance next morning showed that one merchant ship had been hit and damaged in this assault.

Similar missions continued throughout the autumn of 1940 with a few victories for the bombers but 22 Squadron suffered very heavy losses in the process. One of the most gallant exploits of this famous unit was that carried out on the night of the 6th. April, 1941, when four Beauforts went out to try and hit the *Scharnhorst* and *Gneisenau* at Brest after repeated and costly attempts at altitude bombing had failed. Only one of the Beauforts despatched reached the target and this aircraft, gallantly flown by Flying Officer K. Campbell, scored a hit on the *Gneisenau* before being shot down. For this very brave action Campbell was awarded the posthumous Victoria Cross.

Also during 1941, 22 Squadron featured in another gallant attack on German heavy ships when fourteen Beauforts of 22 and 42 Squadrons were despatched to intercept the Pocket Battleship *Lutzow* which was sighted heading north for Trondheim on the 12th. June. At 2.00 a.m. on the 13th., 42 Squadron's aircraft located their target and an attack by Flight Sgt. R.H. Loveitt eighteen minutes later resulted in a hit on the *Lutzow* which left her badly damaged and stopped with a severe list. The German ships had been caught completely by surprise and not a shot was fired for the Beaufort was mistaken for an escorting Ju.88. Two further attacks by 42 Squadron aircraft failed and the battleship was taken in tow by one of her escorting destroyers at 3.20 a.m. and proceeded south back to the haven of Keil. At 4.20 a.m. one of 22 Squadron's Beauforts also made an attack but was shot down without result. *Lutzow* eventually reached Keil on the 14th. and remained there undergoing repairs for six months. Despite a hesitant start after inter-war neglect, the torpedo bomber was proving itself a potent weapon in the hands of the young R.A.F. pilots.

Above: Beauforts stationed at a Royal Air Force base are loaded up with dummy torpedoes.
Below: A torpedo carried by a Beaufort is armed before take-off.

4: Triumph in Battle

In the Mediterranean, from 1940 to 1942, both sides sought to exert control of the sea using land based strike forces. The Italians used their growing numbers of torpedo bombers, based along the sea routes from Gibraltar and Alexandria to Malta, to disrupt British attempts to sustain that island. The British sought to expand their own torpedo bomber forces on Malta in order to operate against the shorter Axis supply routes from Italy and Greece to Libya. The results of these battles were closely interrelated and many times keenly balanced. A tanker destroyed by the *Aerosilurante* before it reached Malta could ground British torpedo bombers operating there and thus enable Italian tankers to reach Rommel's forces advancing on Egypt. The destruction of a German tanker heading for Benghazi would result in lack of fuel for the Panzers and bring them to a halt. The more of the Libyan coastline that was held by the British Army the easier it was to reinforce Malta.

British Operations in the Mediterranean

To attack the Italian battle fleet at Taranto, their main base inside the heel of Italy, had long been an ambition of the Royal Navy. The plan had been put forward before the war when it was considered that the Mediterranean Fleet's solitary aircraft carrier would be able to make the attack before she could be overwhelmed by land-based bombers. Admiral Cunningham had certainly long wished to blow the dust off these plans and put them into effect as Operation 'Judgement' for he was unable to catch the fast Italian ships with his old battleships and an air attack seemed to be the only way to bring them to battle.

The arrival of the new *Illustrious* to support the *Eagle* gave him the opportunity and the attack was planned for Trafalgar Day. However, the *Eagle* had to drop out of the operation, although some of her aircraft were transferred to *Illustrious* so that they could participate. The attack went in on the night of the 11/12th. November, 1940, once it had been confirmed that all six Italian battleships were at Taranto together.

Swordfish from 813, 815, 819 and 824 squadrons took part and they were flown off *Illustrious* in two waves. Only eleven of these aircraft actually carried torpedoes, while the others had bombs and flares. Lieutenant Commander K. Williamson led the first wave and they arrived over the harbour at 11.00 p.m. as the flare markers were released. A formidable baloon barrage and scattered anti-aircraft fire met them but, despite this, all the attacks were pressed home and only one Swordfish was destroyed.

At midnight the second wave reached Taranto, by now a scene of some disorganization. Again anti-aircraft fire was intense but unco-ordinated and these Swordfish also carried out their strikes perfectly, once more losing only a single aircraft to the defences. The result was a famous victory. Twenty-one obsolete aircraft had, in six and half hours flying time, in

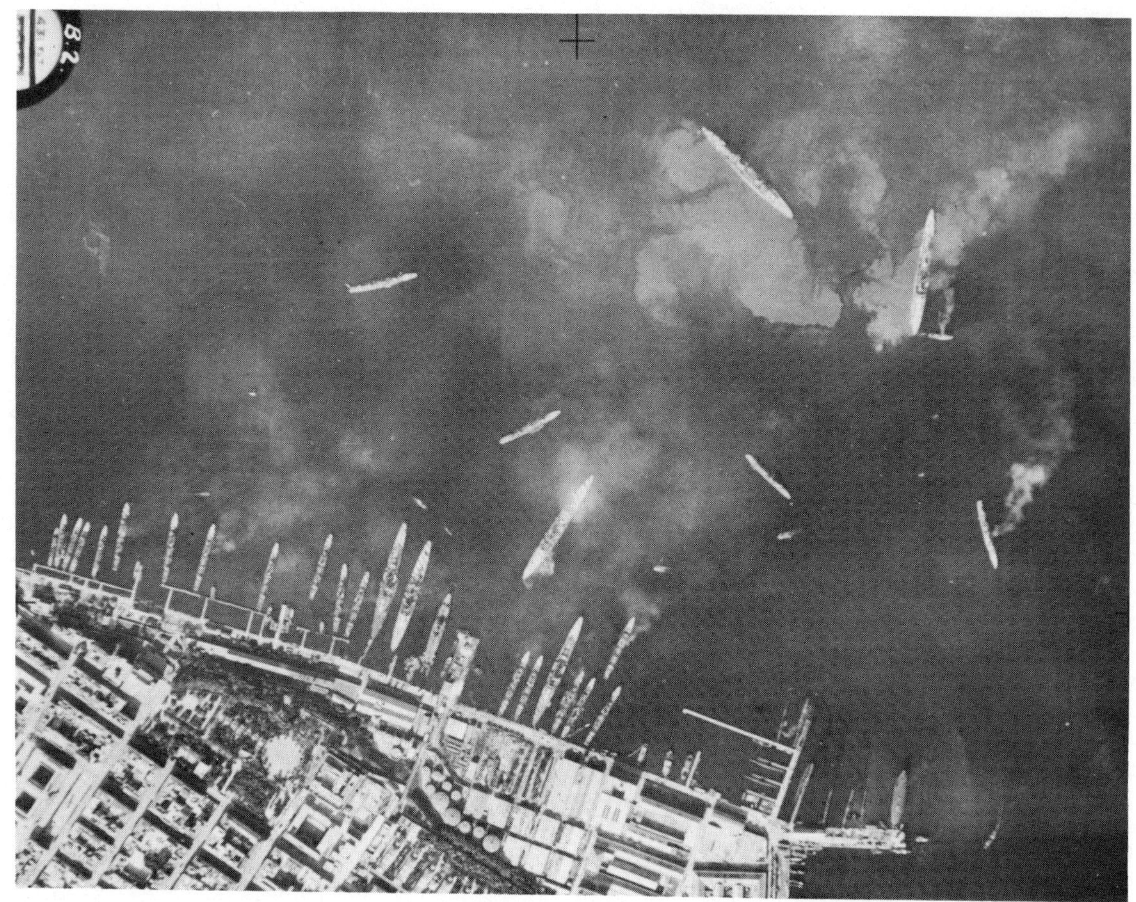

This photograph of the inner harbour at Taranto, taken after the torpedo bombing attack carried out by Swordfish from the *Illustrious,* shows two damaged cruisers of the *Trento* class surrounded by oil on the water.

Admiral Cunningham's words, "inflicted more damage upon the Italian fleet than was inflicted upon the German High Seas Fleet in the daylight action of the Battle of Jutland".

Subsequent reconnaissance showed the extent of the damage these gallant young crews had wrought in the Italian's own front parlour. Three of the six battleships had been torpedoed. The *Cavour* took one hit and sank, the *Diulio* took one hit and sank by the bows and the brand new *Littorio* was hit by no less than three torpedoes and sunk, although she was later raised and repaired. In addition the heavy cruiser *Trento* and the destroyers *Libeccio* and *Pessango* had been hit and two naval auxillaries sunk. On shore, several oil storage tanks were burnt out and seaplane hangars bombed.

Little wonder then that Admiral Cunningham signalled the returning carrier with the understatement, '*Illustrious* manoeuvre well executed". This superb attack will be remembered as the Fleet Air Arm's equivalent to the Battle of Britain. It was a master stroke at a time when the course of the war had taken a far from happy turn for Britain. As well as vindicating the torpedo-bomber concept once and for all, Taranto also marked the greatest achievement of the obsolete little 'Stringbags', although they had yet other glorious chapters to write in the pages of maritime history.

Throughout 1940 and 1941, the British torpedo bombers working from the island of Malta were mainly Fleet Air Arm units. The first of these was 830 squadron formed on 22nd. July, 1940, by Swordfish of 767 Training Squadron. Never at a greater strength than two dozen aircraft at any time, these Swordfish played an important part in harassing the Axis supply lines to North Africa. In a nine month period they despatched an average of no less than 50,000 tons of Italian shipping, and in one month alone they sank 98,000 tons.

In October 1941, these Swordfish were joined and gradually replaced by Albacores of 828 Squadron which began operations that month and continued to operate from Malta until July 1943. Typical of their missions was that carried out in July 1942 when nine Albacores of 828 Squadron flew from Dekheila to attack a convoy off Tripoli with a secret refuelling from Bombay transports some 250 miles behind Axis lines en route.

The first R.A.F. torpedo bomber unit to operate in this theatre of war was 39 Squadron of Beauforts which arrived in the desert towards the end of the year. Co-operating with the Albacores from Malta and Egypt, three Beauforts were sent against a large Italian convoy on 23rd. January, 1942. They managed to score a hit on the 14,000 ton liner *Victoria* and the Albacores later finished her off.

On April 13th., however, another aircraft strike against a large convoy crossing the central Mediterranean turned into a massacre for the R.A.F. Nine Beauforts were despatched, including two from 22 Squadron on their way through Egypt to the Far East. They were to

Right: A reconnaissance photograph taken after the attack on Taranto shows a 23,622 ton battleship of the *Cavour* class beached on the east shore of the outer harbour. Left: A 35,000 ton battleship of the *Littorio* class partially submerged and surrounded by salvage tugs.

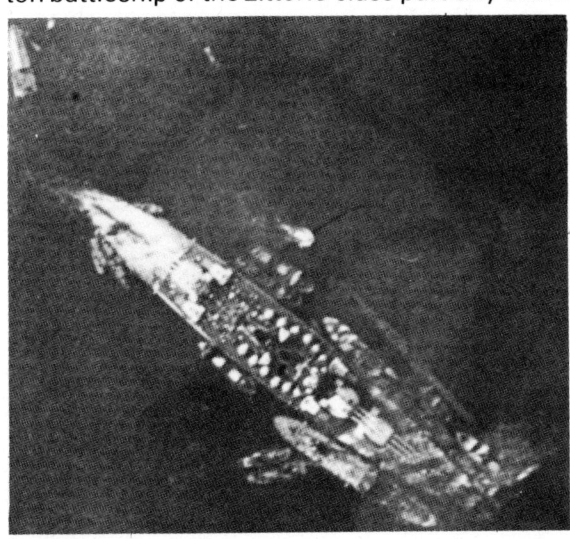

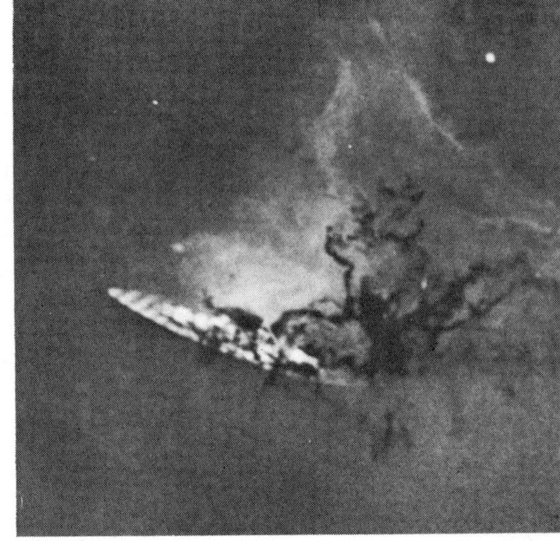

fly from Egypt, attack the convoy and then land at Malta. Four Beaufighters were sent as fighter escort. They found the convoy heavily defended by fighters. They managed to attack and claimed two hits, but they were harrassed all the way to Malta and seven of the Beauforts were lost, only two badly damaged planes reaching the island.

Thirty nine squadron was re-equipped and based at Sidi Barrani and 217 Squadron was flown into Malta to commence operations in June. At dawn on the 15th. June, 1942, the Italian battleships *Littorio* and *Vittoria Veneto,* two heavy and two light cruisers with twelve destroyers, left Taranto to attack an Allied convoy to Malta. To attack this formidable force, the British torpedo bomber forces were far from strong — 39 and 217 Squadrons with Beauforts and four Wellingtons fitted for night torpedo bombing. Of these latter, only one was able to attack, at 3.40 a.m. on the 16th., through a thick smokescreen and her two torpedoes ran wide.

Beauforts of 217 Squadron from Malta were little more accurate. Leaving Malta at 4.00 p.m. they located the Italians at dawn and immediately attacked. The first three aircraft chose the pair of 8-inch cruisers as their targets and Pilot Officer Aldridge scored a single hit on the *Trento.* The remaining six bombers dropped against the battleships and pressed in with outstanding bravery to within 200 yards of their giant opponents, crossing their decks with feet to spare. Despite their claims to have scored two hits on each of the Italian battleships, they had, in fact, missed completely. The Italian fleet was not stopped or even slowed down. Only two of the crews involved had ever before taken part in a real attack on enemy warships before this operation.

Beauforts of 39 Squadron attacked after a high level Liberator attack had claimed to have

A battleship partially sunk by the torpedo attack on Taranto harbour.

A Fairey Swordfish drops a torpedo against a practice target.

scored 23 hits and had in reality scored only one which did no damage. Of the twelve Beauforts despatched, only five, led by Pat Gibbs, ever reached the Italian ships because they were intercepted on the way by German fighters. Of these five all managed to drop at long range but again no hits were scored at all.

Not put off by their earlier failures, both 217 Squadron and the Wellingtons attacked again later, as the Italian fleet was returning to Taranto. The Beauforts failed to find their target but Pilot Officer Hawes of 38 Squadron attacked through thick cloud and gained absolute surprise. Launching both his torpedoes at the *Littorio's* port bow he scored one hit. Again, despite claims, the battleship was not seriously affected by this and it did not even reduce speed and the Italians reached harbour on the 16th. June.

This lack of decisive result dogged the squadrons based at Malta during June and July 1942, and on the 20th. June, a strike by twelve of 217's Beauforts against a small Axis convoy was a complete failure, one aircraft turned back, two were intercepted en-route to the target and the other nine failed to find the convoy at all. The next day nine Beauforts led by Squadron Leader Lynn hit with four torpedoes, and sank, the 7,600 ton *Reichenfels,* at a cost of three aircraft destroyed and the others all damaged.

Twelve Beauforts of 39 Squadron attacked two merchants vessels on 24th. June, damaging one cargo ship, at a cost of three aircraft. This convoy was reassembled and attacked several times by torpedo Wellingtons with no decisive result. A strike on 4th. July by eight Beauforts,

Maintenance work is carried out on a Fairey Albacore stationed at a Malta airfield in 1942.

four of which turned back, resulted in damage to one ship of the three and the loss of three more Beauforts. On 21st. July, six Beauforts from 86 and 217 Squadrons lost yet another three aircraft to damage on a small merchant vessel.

Better results were achieved on August 17th., when the 8,300 ton *Rosalina Pilo* was sunk off Lampedusa and on 20th. and 21st. August attacks made with the loss of three Beauforts resulted in the destruction of the 7,800 ton tanker *Posarica* and, on the 27th., the 1,500 ton *Dielpi,* while Wellingtons sank the *Istria* 5,400 tons. On 30th. August, nine Beauforts struck the *San Andrea,* 5,000 tons and sank her while the tanker *Proserpina,* 5,000 tons and the *Tergestea,* 6,000 tons were both sunk on 26th. October, 1942.

Above and left: A mixed crew of soldiers, sailors and airmen arm and check a R.A.F. Beaufort at Malta before it takes off to attack Axis shipping.

Italian Operations

On 2nd. April, 1941, two SM.79's of 34 *Gruppo* attacked British shipping at Crete and sank the 5,325 ton merchant vessel *Homefield.* On the 18th. April, the tanker *British Science* was torpedoed by Cimicchi of the same unit. In March three SM.79's hit the steamer *Rawnsley.* During the battle for Crete, 281 Squadron made many attacks in co-operation with the Luftwaffe upon Cunningham's fleet defending that island. But the only result achieved was that of sinking the already damaged destroyer *Hereward* after she had been hit by Stukas. In August that year, an attack by three SM.79's piloted by Buscaglia, Graziani and Forzinetti resulted in a hit on the netlayer *Protector* by Graziani but she did not sink.

On 20th. August, 1941, two of 281's aircraft severely damaged the tanker *Turbo,* 4,782 tons, while the next day they attacked a destroyer off Alexandria and claimed a single hit. On 13th. October, three of 281's torpedo bombers made a daylight attack on the British Battle Fleet west of Alexandria, Cesare and Faggioni attacking the battleship *Queen Elizabeth,* while Cimicchi pressed home his attack against the *Barham.* He thought in fact that he had hit her but this claim was not substantiated and a month later she fell victim to *U 331* in the same waters.

On 24th. October, Focacci sank the solitary freighter *Empire Guillemot,* west of Galita Island as she was trying to slip through to Malta. Against the heavily escorted Malta convoys

Italian torpedo bombing "ace", Emilio Buscaglia checks a torpedo being loaded into his SM.79.

Above: The freighter *Empire Guillemot* sinks by the stern after being hit by a torpedo from an SM.79 while sailing to Malta in 1941. Above right: SM.79's attack the Malta convoy *Pedestal.* Below left: The destroyer *Bedouin* sinks after being struck by a torpedo dropped by Buscaglia's SM.79 in an attack on the Malta convoy *Harpoon.*

the Italians also had some successes, although losses grew heavier as the size of the escort grew with each operation.

On 10th. January, 1941, attacks by SM.79's at sea level upon the *Illustrious* during Operation *Excess* played a major part in luring away her defending fighters and thus leaving her open to the concentrated attack by the Stukas who heavily damaged her.

On 23rd July, a force of seven SM.79's attacked the Malta convoy *Substance* heading east

from Gibraltar and achieved absolute surprise. Their torpedoes struck the cruiser *Manchester* in the engine room and disabled three of her four engines. She was towed back to Gibraltar by the destroyers. In the same attack another torpedo hit the destroyer *Fearless* aft in her oil fuel tanks. Ablaze the crippled destroyer lost way and later had to be sunk. The next day the already damaged merchant ship *Sydney Star* was attacked by two SM.79's who pressed home their assault so close that one flew between her masts. They scored a single torpedo hit but the ship still reached Malta.

On 27th. September, 1941, the *Halberd* convoy from Gibraltar to Malta was attacked by twelve BR.20 torpedo bombers. They lost four of their number without scoring any hits. A further attack was made by these aircraft, six pressing in across the destroyer screen and launching their torpedoes at the *Nelson* at mast-head height. Although the great vessel skilfully avoided two of these, a third hit her in her bows, ten feet below the waterline and reduced her speed considerably; but she stayed in line. Further torpedo bomber assaults were made by moonlight that night and the 12,000 ton freighter *Imperial Star* was hit and sank later.

In 1942, the convoys got larger as Malta's plight became more desperate, the Royal Navy's escort grew heavier, but the Axis forces, battleships, cruisers, destroyers, E-boats, dive and torpedo bombers, also vastly increased to their wartime peak. The result was several very fierce encounters. By June the position was extreme and Britain decided to run in two convoys one from each end of the Mediterranean. From the west would come *Harpoon* and from the east *Vigorous*. The Axis replied by sending out strong naval and air forces against both convoys and the result was a massacre. Seventeen merchant ships sailed and only two arrived at Malta. However, the contribution made by the Italian torpedo bombers was limited. In an attack on *Harpoon* Buscaglia hit the already damaged destroyer *Bedouin* with a torpedo and sank her, while the *Liverpool* was hit and towed home for the second time in the war.

The last and greatest of all the Malta convoy operations was *Pedestal* which took place on August from the west only. I have already written at length to describe this famous battle*, and so here will only summarise the part played by the torpedo bombers. Fourteen merchant ships escorted by two battleships, three aircraft carriers, seven cruisers and two dozen destroyers formed the convoy. The Axis torpedo bomber forces consisted of fifty nine SM.79's from 130 *Gruppo,* 254, 255, 278 and 281 squadrons, sixteen SM.84's of 130 *Gruppo* and six Heinkel He.111's from 11/KG.26 which had been undergoing training at Grossetto.

The first torpedo bomber attack was by the six German aircraft at dusk on the 11th. August against the *Victorious,* without result. The major air assault took place the next day and at 12.40 p.m. the first wave of bombers reached the convoy. These were ten S.84's of 132 *Stormo* carrying *motobombas.* These were dropped in the path of the ships to force them to turn away, thus opening up the convoy's defensive ranks and enabling the torpedo bombers to penetrate the screen of warships to reach the merchantmen. It was a good plan but lack of co-ordination resulted in the subsequent waves arriving too late to take advantage of this. They were met with heavy anti-aircraft fire and the fleet's fighters with the result that no hits were scored. One SM.79 and two SM.84's were lost in this attack.

The second assault took place at 6.00 p.m. and again although co-ordination was better the only hit scored by the Italian torpedo bombers, twenty-two of which took part, was that scored on the destroyer *Foresight.* She was struck aft in her steering compartment and after a long attempt to tow her home she had to be sunk.

At dusk, the six Heinkels returned to attack twice, hitting the convoy as it tried to force the narrows under heavy submarine attack. Two He.III's caught the steamer *Deucalion* off the Cani Rocks and, coasting in with their engines cut off, achieved surprise, hitting her with two torpedoes. She blew up and later sank. Another Heinkel put a torpedo into the *Brisbane Star* but she managed after a while to carry on independently and reached Malta. Another torpedo from one of the German aircraft struck the *Clan Ferguson* which blew up with a tremendous explosion and sank with heavy loss of life.

Many merchant ships were badly damaged by E-boat attacks during the night and in the morning the Axis torpedo bombers were kept busy finishing off these unfortunates. The *Wairangi, Santa Elisa* and *Almeria Lykes* were sent to the bottom. But determined attacks by SM.79's against the lone tanker *Ohio* failed, due to a great part by the spirited defence put up by her escorts, one of which, the destroyer *Pathfinder,* steamed head-on into a formation of six SM.79's and drove them off. Thus ended the largest air/sea battle of the Mediterranean

British Operations in the Atlantic

The faithful old Swordfish continued to operate during 1941 and on into 1942 in their original torpedo role and added yet more laurels to their enviable record. In the North Atlantic in May 1941, the great German battleship *Bismarck* broke out and, after destroying the *Hood* and damaging the *Prince of Wales,* looked certain to reach France and safety before the Home Fleet could stop her. Everything depended on the Swordfish squadrons embarked in the brand new carrier *Victorious* and Force 'H's' carrier *Ark Royal.*

* *Pedestal;* The Malta Convoy of August 1942: Peter C. Smith; William Kimber: 1970.

Obsolete Swordfish such as these were used by Lieutenant Commander Esmonde's squadron in their heroic attacks on the *Bismarck.*

At 10.00 p.m. on the 24th. May, Lieutenant Commander E. Esmonde led nine Swordfish from *Victorious* and flew through rain squalls to make a night attack on their target. At 11.27 p.m. they made radar contact and sighted *Bismarck*. They attacked soon after midnight and managed to score a single hit, but as this was on her amidships armoured belt it did no damage.

Contact was then lost for a considerable time but when it was re-established only the *Ark Royal* stood between the *Bismarck* and sanctuary. At 2.50 p.m. on the 25th., fourteen Swordfish left *Ark Royal's* flight deck which was rearing and plunging in heavy seas. At 3.50 p.m. they made their attacks, but it was against the light cruiser *Sheffield* of Force 'H' and not the *Bismarck*. Fortunately the cruiser avoided the torpedoes and held her fire. She was also able to notify her attackers that their torpedoes were exploding prematurely due to a fault in their magnetic pistols. The second strike had these replaced by contact pistols. It says very little for the warship identification ability of even seasoned Fleet Air Arm pilots when they could mistake a 9,000 ton cruiser with twin funnels and triple mountings for the

Armourers load a Swordfish with a torpedo.

42,000 ton single funnelled, twin mountings, *Bismarck,* especially when *Sheffield* had accompanied them to sea for weeks.

The second wave left the *Ark Royal* at 7.10 p.m. and comprised fifteen Swordfish. These Swordfish from 810, 818 and 820Squadrons were led by Lieutenant Commander T.P. Coode. They first located the *Sheffield* who then carefully re-directed them to the *Bismarck*. They attacked at 10.47 p.m. and scored two hits during the next 38 minutes. One was on the armoured belt; the other was aft, a vital hit, which disabled her steering gear and jammed her rudders. She was now doomed and went down under the guns of the Home Fleet the next day.

Esmonde and the Swordfish of 825 squadron also featured in the last gallant torpedo bomber attack mounted by the 'Stringbags'. The *Ark Royal* was sunk in November 1941 and 825 Squadron was re-formed under Esmonde at Manston in Kent. Here they were held in readiness for a night attack on the battle-cruisers *Scharnhorst* and *Gneisenau* and the heavy cruiser *Hipper* if they should run up the Channel as was expected. The Channel dash did in fact take place, but by day and not by night. Esmonde and his six obsolete torpedo bombers were flung in against them on 12th. February, 1942. They located the three German giants ten miles off Ramsgate, surrounded by escorting warships and with the sky black with the Luftwaffe. None the less, the six Swordfish, with minimum fighter cover, attacked although they knew that their chances were just about nil. They attacked in line astern and all were shot down within a few minutes by the warships' anti-aircraft guns, without scoring any hits. Esmonde was awarded a posthumous Victoria Cross. Of the eighteen pilots and crew, only five survived the attack.

The R.A.F. then sent in what torpedo bombers they had. Squadron-Leader George Taylor, D.F.C., led seven of 217 Squadron's Beauforts against the German ships. Two failed to find the target, one was shot down and the others attacked bravely but did not hit. Nine of 42 Squadron's Beauforts also attacked without result, as did 242 of the R.A.F.'s Bomber Command. Of the bombers, only 39 actually found the German ships and they did not hit with a single bomb. The final torpedo bomber attack was mounted by twelve Beauforts of 86, 22 and 217 Squadrons led by Wing-Commander Charles Flood, but they also failed to locate the German ships which reached Germany with only mine damage.

The comparative failure of the slow Beauforts in this and many other attacks, coupled with heavy losses, led ultimately to its replacement and the introduction into the R.A.F. of the Beaufighter as a torpedo aircraft. The Mark 1C Beaufighter, equipped with two 1,425 horse power Bristol Hercules XI engines was fitted with torpedo installations. When equipped with this aircraft, the R.A.F. was finally to play an effective role against shipping.

The Swordfish had a record without equal in the torpedo bomber role but after the massacre in the Channel in 1942 it was obvious that this old aircraft had had it's day as a torpedo bomber. But it's duties were far from complete and Swordfish became used as general-purpose anti-submarine aircraft, armed with rockets and depth charges and operating from escort carriers in the Atlantic and on the Russia convoys. The Swordfish carried on well past D-Day before being completely phased out of service.

This photograph shows the first Beaufighter to be adapted for torpedo bombing. The "Torbeau" replaced the Beaufort as the R.A.F.'s front line torpedo bomber.

German Operations

As we have seen earlier the Luftwaffe was backward in developing torpedo bombing and with ample evidence before them of its effectiveness their plans had to be re-cast. By 1941, the Luftwaffe had started to take interest in the torpedo bomber but its efforts were not welcomed by the Navy. Much of the data already gained on the use of aerial torpedoes was held back by the Navy, the Technical Office was not assisted and independent work with private firms was hindered.

None the less the Luftwaffe set up a torpedo bombing school at Grossenbrode, and, by the autumn of 1941, had reached the conclusion that the Heinkel He.111 and the Junkers Ju.88 were both suitable types for torpedo bombing. Initial work was commenced with the He.111 H6 variant and this became the main work horse of the Luftwaffe's torpedo bomber force.

The He.111 H6 could be adapted to carry two F4B torpedoes externally. The Luftwaffe were so confident of its suitability that several of these aircraft were sent out to Athens to operate in the Eastern Mediterranean. However, owing to lack of torpedoes or non-arrival of the warheads these operations had to be abandoned.

In December 1941, a direct demand was made that the Luftwaffe should assume control of aerial torpedo development in both Germany and Italy, and further, that experimental stations should be set up, naval personnel absorbed and a Commissioner appointed to control all aspects. This was immediately granted.

The anti-shipping expert Harlinghausen became the Commissioner and plans were made to set up a force of 230 torpedo bombers. As the Grossenbrode base in the Baltic was

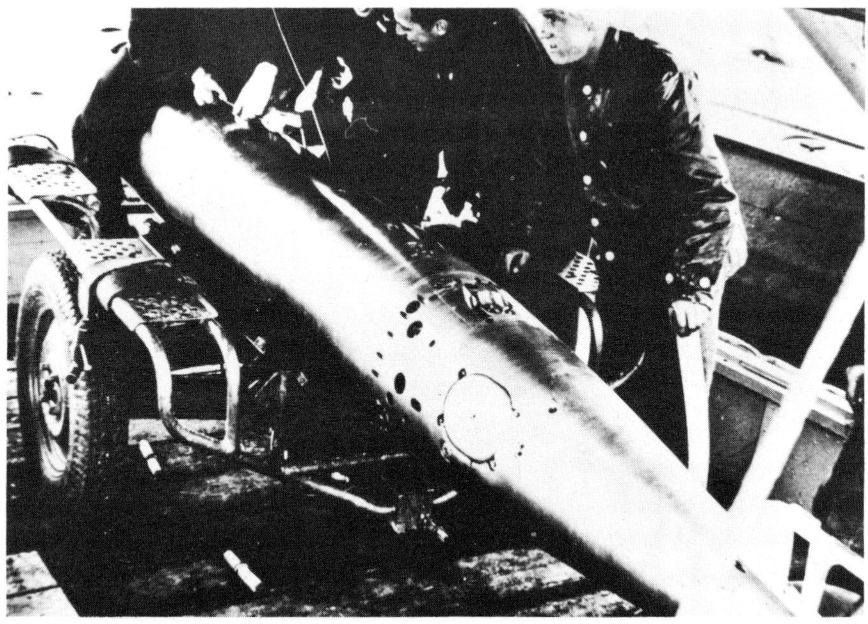

German armourers work on a torpedo.

This sequence of three photographs shows a Heinkel He.111 dropping one of its two torpedoes.

wintered in, the training and development unit was moved down to Grosseto, south of Leghorn in Italy. There, training could continue at full speed and close liaison with the *Aerosilurante* could be maintained.

The crack anti-shipping squadrons of KG.26, based in Norway, were the first units to be converted to this new role. By the end of April 1942, the first twelve crews of I/KG.26 had been trained and were equipped with their He.111 H6's. They were based at the specially built airfields of Banak and Bardufoss in north Norway, where they could menace convoys to Russia. The whole of I/KG.26, forty two aircraft, was ready by June 1942, while III/KG.26 was undergoing conversion to the Junkers Ju.88A 17 for a similar role. By July 1942, some 42 Heinkels and 33 Junkers, these latter based at Rennes in France, were ready for operations. In the remarkably short time of eight months the Luftwaffe had, from scratch almost, developed the most effective torpedo bomber striking force in Europe.

The first successful torpedo bomber attack that this powerful and confident new arm of the Luftwaffe made was that carried out against the ill-fated convoy PQ.17 when it was still unbroken and strongly guarded and heading for Soviet Russia packed with arms, ammunition and equipment. An earlier attack, on PQ.16, had shown that high level dive bombing by orthodox Ju.88's coupled with the launching of torpedoes from 30 feet, the normal

Left: A Heinkel He. 111, stationed at Grossetto in Italy carrying two practice torpedoes. Right: A Junkers Ju.88 taking off, armed with two torpedoes.

launching height, would greatly upset the convoy escorts. Therefore, these combined attacks were practiced at length while the actual torpedo bombing technique was developed. The torpedo bombers were to approach in a wide line abreast, known as the 'Golden Comb' *(Goldene Zange),* launching all their missiles together in a twilight assault with the convoy silhouetted against the setting sun.

PQ.17 consisted of thirty four merchant ships with a strong escort of destroyers and lesser ships, a covering cruiser squadron and the Home Fleet, with two battleships, a carrier, cruisers and destroyers, in far distant support. It was the German Navy's torpedo bombers of 1/906 squadron however which made the first impact on this doomed convoy. At 4.50 p.m. on the 3rd. July one of the floatplanes which had been shadowing the ships, cut its engines and at a height of only 30 feet glided gently in over the convoy and released its two torpedoes before soaring safely away. One of the torpedoes struck the 7,197 ton *Christopher Newport* which was promptly abandoned and was later finished off by a submarine.

The afternoon of the 4th. July saw the Luftwaffe make their initial strike. All three Staffeln of I/KG.26 took part in this assault from Bardufoss, a total of 23 Heinkels. The Ju.88's of KG.30 were to co-operate with a bombing attack. This assault was led by the commander of the I/KG.26's 3rd. Staffel, Captain Eicke. The 23 Heinkels attacked in two waves and were opposed by massed fire, most of it wild, from the convoy, and steadier and more accurate fire from the escorting warships. None of this was very effective but with the convoy at the time was the U.S. destroyer *Wainwright* better equipped than British vessels for air attack. This ship, like the *Pathfinder* during *Pedestal,* took the novel but wise course of steaming directly out towards the incoming torpedo bombers to break them up. The wave she thus engaged consisted of about ten aircraft and of these, only one, piloted by Lieutenant

Kaumeyer, bored in over the destroyer and past her to launch one torpedo before being shot down.

On the starboard quarter of the convoy the other Heinkels were allowed to press in toward their targets, some launching at 6,000 yards range while others, including Eicke, pressed even closer. These, the outstanding example being Lieutenant Hennemann, crossed right through the convoy. For a total loss of three aircraft, hits were made on three ships; *William Hooper,* (7,177 tons), *Navarino* (4,841 tons) and *Azerbaigen* (6,114 tons).

The success of this attack led the Luftwaffe at the time (and some British "experts" since) to assume that this torpedo bomber attack had caused the break up of PQ.17. However, it was the threat of the *Tirpitz* which did this, but none the less it was a gallant debut.

An attack on a convoy off the Scilly Isles on the night of the 3rd. August by the Rennes aircraft was not such a good attack, but the work of II/KG.26 against *Pedestal* as already described the same month was outstanding. However, the greatest Luftwaffe victory was once again against a Russia bound convoy. This took place on October 17th, 1942 when the convoy PQ.18 came under attack. The Luftwaffe units in Norway had reached a total strength of 92 aircraft with the arrival in the zone of III/KG.26 with a strength of 35 Ju.88's. Warnings had already been received that PQ.18 would be accompanied by an escort carrier with single engined fighters embarked. This would greatly add to the torpedo bombers' problems. The decision was taken therefore that this carrier should be made one of the prime targets of the attacks. Should she be sunk or damaged the rest of the convoy would fall easily.

In fact, the Royal Navy was equally determined to provide the maximum defence for this convoy, and, as in the case of *Pedestal* in the Mediterranean in August, both sides reached their peak strengths at the same time. The carrier provided was the small escort carrier

Avenger with Sea Hurricane fighters and Swordfish embarked. A new anti-aircraft cruiser, the *Scylla* with eight 4.5 inch guns, was the flagship of Rear Admiral Bob Burnett and there was a very strong 'Fighting Destroyer Escort' in case German heavy ships should intervene. These, together with the close escort destroyers amounted to no less than eighteen ships. Further heavy anti-aircraft firepower was added with the A.A. ships *Alynbank* and *Ulster Queen* while there were additional small escorts, corvettes, minesweepers and trawlers. This massive force was designed to give protection to the convoy which consisted of forty fully laden transports bound for Murmansk to supply the Russian armies fighting desperately around Stalingrad.

The German torpedo bombers struck the convoy immediately after the defending Sea Hurricanes had been skilfully lured away by bombing carried out by the Ju.88's of KG.30. The result was devastating. For the first time the 'Golden Comb' was used to maximum effect and the British escorts described their first appearance at 3.00 p.m. in line abreast, thirty feet above the water as like 'a huge flight of nightmare locusts'.

The convoy was in block formation of ten columns each of four ships, although there were already some gaps where the U-boats had been active in the preceeding days. The torpedo bombers attacked from the starboard side of the formation and the Commodore signalled the convoy to carry out an emergency turn of 45 degrees to starboard. The merchantmen, however, were too confused in the face of such an attack to carry out this and remained steaming steadily at right-angles to the oncoming bombers.

The torpedo bombers pressed in boldly through an enormous barrage to drop their missiles with deadly accuracy. Only five bombers fell to the massed fire of the escorting warships and aircraft. The others released their torpedoes, some seventy-four in all, and were soon over the horizon as their missiles struck home.

Of the seven ships in the two starboard columns, six were hit, one blowing up with a colossal explosion, the others emitting great clouds of steam and smoke as they lurched beneath the ocean. Further torpedoes passed into the heart of the massed ranks of steamers and two more ships went down. It was a disaster, for at a cost of five aircraft the men of KG.26 had, in eight minutes, sunk eight heavily-laden steamers, a quarter of the convoy. The ships destroyed in this attack were the *Empire Beaumont, Empire Stevenson, John Penn, Wacosta, Afrikander, Oregonian, Macbeth* and *Sukhona.*

Two further attacks by nine and twelve torpedo bombers later that day did not score any further hits and two bombers were destroyed. It was plain that the first attack was the high-water mark of the Luftwaffe's efforts. Two more attacks were mounted on the 14th. by twenty and twenty-five torpedo bombers, most of which concentrated on the *Avenger* and other escorts, but her Sea Hurricanes managed to intercept them this time and with the loss of three of their own number, and aided by the warship's barrage, they claimed to have destroyed a further 21 Heinkels and Junkers. Despite this the torpedo bombers again got through to the convoy and hit the ammunition ship *Mary Luckenbach* in the starboard column which blew up with a great explosion.

On the 15th., only small attacks were made, without effect, by ordinary bombers, and on the 16th. a determined assault by a mere twelve of KG.26's aircraft penetrated right into the convoy and hit the *Kentucky,* which was later finished off by dive bombers. The ten ships

The *Navarino* bound for Russia in the Arctic convoy P.Q.17 falls victim to a missile from a German torpedo bomber.

destroyed in these October battles marked the swan-song of the Luftwaffe's torpedo bomber forces in the Arctic for in November they were all withdrawn to bases at Grosseto, Catania and Cagliari. The orders, which came through on the 2nd. November, were given because it was thought that the torpedo bombers would have more scope in attacking shipping in the Mediterranean than in northern waters. The transfer of the *Gruppen* took only five to nine days, and one *Staffel* managed it in 48 hours.

Japanese and United States Operations in the Pacific

When Japan entered World War II in December, 1941, the United States Pacific Fleet, moored at Pearl Harbor on the Hawaiian island of Oahu, was the only Allied force in the Pacific which posed any serious threat to Japanese ambitions. On 7th. December, an air armada, launched from Vice-Admiral Nagumo's task force of six carriers and two battleships carried out a devastating surprise attack on the United States fleet.

In the first wave of 183 aircraft were forty Kate's led by Lieutenant Commander Shigeharu Murata of the *Akagi.* When the attack had first been planned, the use of torpedo bombers was opposed due to the shallowness of the water at Pearl Harbor but Murata overcame all these difficulties. Achieving complete surprise, the attack was launched at 7.49 a.m. Only five Kate's were lost in this attack. The 159 Japanese aircraft assigned to actually attack the American fleet left behind them the battleships *Arizona, California,* and *West Virginia* sunk, *Oklahoma* capsized, *Nevada, Maryland, Pennysylvania* and *Tennessee* damaged, along with three light cruisers, three destroyers and many auxillaries.

Within three days the Japanese Navy achieved what no other air force of any nation had done; the destruction of two capital ships at sea. This came about when Admiral Tom Philips bravely sortied north from Singapore into the South China Sea with *Prince of Wales, Repulse* and three destroyers in order to destroy reported Japanese invasion fleets heading towards Malaya. The R.A.F. had pulled it's fighters back to the island and the fleet had no carrier. Even so, Philips knew that the nearest bases available to the Japanese were those handed over by the Vichy authorities around Saigon, 400 nautical miles away, and, it is said, that Philips believed that no torpedo bomber in the world at that time had such a range!

The British squadron was sighted heading north on the afternoon of December 9th. and the message was received at Saigon at 4.00 p.m. that day. Here was based the 22nd. Air Flotilla of the 11th. Air Fleet. The *Genzan* Squadron under the command of Captain Sonokawa consisted of Betty bombers and they were loading up in preparation for an attack on Singapore. They hastily re-armed with torpedoes and took off at 6.00 p.m. After quartering the likely course of the British ships, the *Genzan* Squadron returned at midnight without sighting them.

At 6.00 a.m. ten *Genzan* Betty's armed with bombs took up the hunt again. At 7.00 a.m.

Left: A Nakajima B5N2 "Kate" is cheered on its way as it takes off from a Japanese aircraft carrier. Right: Smoke pours from the *Arizona* in "battleship row" after the Japanese attack on Pearl Harbor.

the main striking force, of 27 high level bombers and 61 torpedo bombers, Betty's and Nell's, from the *Genzan, Mikoro* and *Kanoya* Squadrons,also set off to attack the two British heavy ships. At 11.00 a.m. on 10th. December they were sighted, and half an hour later the assault started. The torpedo bombing analysis shows that the *Genzan* Squadron dropped seven torpedoes against *Repulse* of which four were hits, the *Kanoya* Squadron launched twenty torpedoes, with ten hits and the *Mikoro* Squadron hit with four of their seven torpedoes against the elderly battle-cruiser.

Against the brand-new *Prince of Wales* were dropped nine torpedoes from the *Genzan* squadron, four of which were claimed as hits, and six of the *Kanoya* Squadron, four of which were claimed hits. Although the numbers of hits actually made was far less than those claimed it mattered little for the result was the same. A surprise for the British was that the Japanese torpedoes were dropped, and ran perfectly true, from a height of 300 to 400 feet. Current British practice had been for an approach to be made at 30 to 40 feet. This high approach nullified much of the close-range A.A. fire.

The *Repulse* went down at 12.33 p.m. and the *Prince of Wales* sank with Admiral Philips at 1.20 p.m. The cost to the Japanese Navy was a mere four aircraft. Having sunk the American and British battleships with a combination of high level, dive and torpedo bombing attacks the Japanese Navy moved south-west quickly overrunning Allied positions. After their surface fleet defeated an allied squadron in the Java Sea, Nagumo's carriers sortied into the Indian Ocean and her dive bombers sank the carrier *Hermes,* the heavy cruisers *Cornwall* and *Dorsetshire,* the destroyer *Vampire* and others. Nell's from shore bases despatched the American seaplane carrier *Langley* south of Java.

In these victories the torpedo bombers were not called upon. To protect their southern flank and prepare a springboard for the invasion of Australia, the Japanese thrust towards

Torpedoes strike home on United States battleships moored off Ford Island, Pearl Harbor.

New Guinea and this resulted in the first carrier to carrier air/sea battle of the war, the Battle of the Coral Sea, which took place on 7th./8th. May, 1942. The Japanese had three carriers available, the large *Shokaku* and *Zuikaku* and the small *Shoho.* The Allies had a cruiser force and the carriers *Lexington* and *Yorktown.*

At 6.10 a.m. on the 7th., the large Japanese carriers launched a striking force, which included 24 Kate's against a U.S. force. In the subsequent assault the oiler *Neosho* and the destroyer *Sims* were sunk quickly by bombs and torpedoes. In return the Americans struck back with torpedo and dive bombing attacks on the *Shoho.* Ten Devastators from *Lexington* made their runs at 11.10 a.m. but the Japanese carrier managed to avoid all their missiles. At 11.25 a.m. however strikes from *Yorktown* bored through what was left of *Shoho's* defences with terrible effect. Hit by thirteen bombs and seven torpedoes the carrier went down at 11.36 a.m.

Admiral Takagi now despatched a strike force which included fifteen Kate torpedo bombers against the American carriers. These aircraft flew off at 4.50 p.m. but they failed to make an attack. Next day, 8th. May, at 8.25 a.m. the Japanese launched a 99-plane combined strike from *Shokaku* and *Zuikaku.* Meanwhile the *Lexington* had despatched her own bombers. The U.S. aircraft left at 8.15 a.m. but torpedoes launched at *Shokaku* were all at long range and not effective, but she did suffer bomb damage. Twenty Devastators attacked, and three were shot down.

At 11.18 a.m. the Japanese attacked the *Lexington* in two torpedo bomber groups, hitting with a torpedo on each side. *Yorktown* was also attacked but no torpedo hits were obtained, but again the dive bombers were more successful. *Lexington* later sank but the *Yorktown* was repaired at high speed at Pearl Harbor and was ready for the next battle; neither of the Japanese carriers were.

On 4th. June, 1942, came the decisive Battle of Midway. The Japanese sailed their main strength against this strategic island. Discounting the diversionary attacks against the Aleutians, they had a total of four heavy carriers, with the First Carrier Striking Force, *Akagi, Kaga, Hiryu* and *Soryu,* plus the light carriers with the Main Body, the *Hosho* and *Zuiho*. Each of the four big carriers had aboard 21 Kate torpedo bombers, commanded respectively by Lieutenant Commander Shigeharu Murata and Lieutenants Ichiro Kitajima, Rokuro Kikuchi and Heijiro Abe.

The first Japanese wave was launched at 4.45 a.m. and consisted of 108 aircraft to strike at Midway Island, but it included no torpedo bombers. The second wave was readied in case the American fleet appeared. This contained a total of 36 Kate torpedo bombers, (eighteen each from the *Akagi* and *Kaga* led by Lieutenant Commander Shigeharu Murata of *Akagi).*

In fact the Americans were forewarned and ready and waiting. Task Force 16 had the

Below right: A destroyer alongside the sinking *Prince of Wales* attempts to take off survivors.
Below left: This Japanese reconnaissance photograph shows the *Repulse* and the *Prince of Wales* sinking after being torpedoed and bombed by Japanese "Betty's" and "nell's".

carriers *Hornet* and *Enterprise* under Rear Admiral R.A. Spruance and Task Force 17 had the *Yorktown* under Rear Admiral Fletcher. Both forces were screened only by cruisers and destroyers. They were some two hundred miles north-east of Midway. The first torpedo bomber attack made by the Americans was by six Navy Avengers and four Army B.26 Marauders from Midway Island which reached the Japanese fleet at 7.00 a.m. Of the ten, only one Avenger and two Marauders ever returned to Midway and no hits were obtained for their sacrifice. Further attacks by Army B.17's and Marine Dauntless dive bombers from Midway were equally unsuccessful. The returning Japanese strike force landed at 8.36 a.m. and the U.S. carriers were first sighted at 7.28 a.m. *Akagi* and *Kaga's* torpedo bombers were being re-armed with bombs for another attack against Midway Island. They had therefore to be struck down yet again and armed once more with torpedoes. But before they could be despatched the American carriers struck hard.

Both *Hornet* and *Enterprise* despatched fourteen torpedo bombers, 33 dive bombers and ten fighters at 7.00 a.m. and began their attacks at 9.30 a.m. The first of these consisted of fifteen torpedo bombers of Hornet's VTB-8, led by Lieutenant Commander J.C. Waldron. Set upon by fifty Zero fighters guarding the fleet every one was shot down and destroyed and of their gallant crews there was only one survivor, Ensign G.H. Gay. They were followed a few minutes later by fourteen torpedo bombers from *Enterprise* and they too took a beating, eleven being shot down, and the torpedoes of the other three all missing their targets. Then came twelve torpedo bombers from *Yorktown* and they too were decimated without result. The sacrifice of the U.S. torpedo bombers at Midway was terrible, of the forty-one which took part only six returned to their carriers.

But it was not a vain sacrifice for the torpedo bombers brought the bulk of the defending

Left: Japanese torpedo bombers take off from an aircraft carrier. Above right: United States Navy Gruman Avengers queue for take off on a carrier.

Japanese Zero's down to sea-level. As a result, the Dauntless dive bombers were able to break through to score a devastating series of direct hits on the fragile wooden flight decks of the *Akagi, Kaga* and *Soryu,* all three of which sank with heavy loss of life. Only the *Hiryu* remained to get in a return strike but she only had dive bombers available. These damaged *Yorktown* in an attack at noon. A second strike of ten Kate's was sent off at 1.30 p.m. under the command of Lieutenant Joichi Tomonaga. They attacked at 2.40 p.m. and scored two torpedo hits, but only five of the Kate's returned from the attack. The U.S. dive bombers then attacked and sank the *Hiryu* and the cruiser *Mikuma.* The battle was now virtually over for the Japanese battleships had been left too far astern to be able to bring their overwhelming fire power in play. It was a major defeat for the Japanese, and a distinct turning point in the Pacific war.

Despite the appalling debut at Midway, the Grumman Avenger TBF-1 went on to become the most successful carrier-born torpedo bomber of the war. Designed by William T Schwendler to replace the Devastator, it was a three-seater, all-metal monoplane, powered by a single 1,850 horse power Wright Cyclone engine. It had a maximum speed of 259 m.p.h. and had a range of 1,000 miles. Fitted with a power-operated gun turret the Avenger could carry a 22-inch torpedo internally. 10,000 were built, and of these 1,000 were supplied to the Fleet Air Arm under Lease Lend.

The Royal Navy however used this outstanding torpedo bomber as a dive bomber and

A United States Navy Avenger drops a torpedo.

rejected the true dive bomber types available, like the Dauntless and the Helldiver. As a dive bomber the Avenger equipped fifteen line squadrons in the Royal Navy. The U.S. Navy used them mainly in their correct role throughout the war, although it proved itself equally adaptable for mine-laying or anti-submarine work with depth charges, and ship attacks with rockets, as well as bombing.

5: Decline and Abandonment

Great Britain

In 1942, the Royal Navy was still heavily reliant on obsolete types like the Swordfish, but they were being phased out, although still operating from escort carriers.

In 1942, the Fleet Air Arm was supplied with a monoplane replacement, the Fairey Barracuda. This exceedingly ugly aeroplane was first developed as a replacement for the Albacore in 1937 and made its first flight at the end of 1940 becoming thus the first monoplane torpedo bomber designed for the Royal Navy. The Mark I, of which less than thirty were built, did not appear until May 1942, and it was not until as late as August 1942, some five years after work had commenced, that the Mark II considered suitable for operational service, was to appear.

It was a three-seater, high-winged monoplane, powered by one 1,640 horse power Rolls Royce Merlin 32 engine which gave a maximum speed of 228 m.p.h. It could carry a single 1,620 pound torpedo externally at a range of 686 miles only. Span was 49 feet 2 inches, length 35 feet 9 inches and height 15 feet 4 inches. Although originally designed as a torpedo

A pilot watches while the torpedo carried by his Swordfish is armed aboard the United States built escort carrier *H.M.S. Battler.*

Fleet Air Arm Fairey Barracudas fly in echelon formation. The Barracuda was used more as a dive bomber than a torpedo bomber.

bomber, it was not an outstanding success in that role. Like the British Avenger, it was used as a dive bomber during most of its brief wartime service with the Fleet Air Arm, a role for which it was more fitted, and one which it performed very well. The most outstanding achievements of the Barracuda were the superb dive bombing attacks on the *Tirpitz* in 1944. They were employed in the East Indies in the same role, as well as in anti-shipping strikes off the Norwegian coast. For these latter operations, the heavy, clumsy Barracudas were power-assisted off the tiny flight decks by rocket-assisted take-offgear. Rarely used as a torpedo bomber, and inferior by far to the Avenger anyway, the Barracuda was typical of the delayed hybrids which came from British designers of this period.

Not surprisingly then it was superceded in the main attack carriers of the British Pacific Fleet in 1945 by the superior Avenger, large numbers of which became available in 1944/45. These formed the backbone of the B.P.F.'s air striking forces in the final drive on Japan. At their peak Avengers were operational with no less than ten Fleet Air Arm squadrons.

United States Avenger torpedo bombers in Royal Navy service as the 'Tarpon', are armed before taking off on a dawn attack.

The Royal Air Force too was slowly re-equipping. In June 1942, Coastal Command had only two squadrons of torpedo bombers, 68 and 415. Although it was fully realised that the torpedo was the best weapon against warships, both aircraft and torpedoes remained in short supply. With all the Beauforts operating in the Mediterranean (42, 86 and 217Squadrons) at this time, the old Hampden bombers were equipped as torpedo carriers and formed into 144, 415, 455 and 489 squadrons in July 1942. The Hampdens were slow, sluggish and vulnerable, although they did have the one virtue of reasonable range. The lack of success achieved at this time was so great that the R.A.F. finally equipped the superb Beaufighter to carry torpedoes. During the period January to July 1942 for example the R.A.F. made 6,617 anti-shipping sorties and only achieved the sinking of thirty small ships with the loss of 195 aircraft.

The specially equipped Beaufighters, known as 'Torbeaus', first joined 254 Squadron in November 1942 and went into operation with an attack on a German convoy off the Dutch coast on the 20th. of that month. The result was an expensive failure. Two squadrons of

Above: A Bristol Beaufighter adapted for torpedo bombing stands ready for take off. Below: A "Torbeau" Beaufighter with D-Day invasion stripes.

fighters, Beaufighters and Spitfires, accompanied 254 Squadron from its North Coates base on this strike against a fifteen-ship convoy located off the Frisian Islands.

The 'Torbeaus' lost three of their number destroyed and four others damaged by flak and the escorting Fw.190's, without scoring a single hit on the convoy. As a direct result of this action the new Torbeaus were withdrawn from fighting and did not venture out again until a detailed training programme had been undertaken, which lasted until April 1943.

With the continued heavy losses suffered for slight returns on day operations, the R.A.F. followed the Navy into considering night torpedo bombing. For a time during 1942, the Fleet Air Arm made available to Coastal Command several Albacores for this duty. Also, as has already been described, some old Wellington bombers were hastily converted to the torpedo bomber role at Malta, and this was followed by more careful adaptations.

The famous old 'Wimpey' had been Bomber Command's main work-horse for the early part of the war and was now replaced in front line service by four engined aircraft. However, it still had good range and capacity for its new task.

The Wellington was a twin-engined, high-winged, monoplane. It was powered by two Bristol Pegasus XVIII engines and had a maximum speed of 255 m.p.h. with a range of 1,325 miles. The Mark VIII was specially developed for Coastal Command operations and was fitted with A.S.V. Mark II search radar. It was known as the 'Stickleback' because of the row of aerials along the aircraft's back. A later mark, the G.R.XI, was intended as a torpedo bomber, carrying the A.S.V. Mark III.

It has a few successes, the most spectacular being the exploits of the 44 Squadron Wellingtons during night operations during the abortive Aegean Campaign of autumn 1943. On the night of the 18th. October, four of these Wellingtons sank the large German steamer *Sinfra,* and this was hailed as a great victory for 2,000 troops were drowned. Unfortunately for

R.A.F. "Torbeaus" and cannon-firing Beaufighters attack a German convoy. The aircraft from which the photograph was taken is about to drop a torpedo against the merchantman at **1**. The aircraft at **2** has already dropped its torpedo (**3**), against the ship at **4**. The ships carry barrage balloons (**5** and **6**). Bombs fall in the water (**7** and **8**). At **9**, cannon fire rakes the water where a ship has taken evasive action.

post-war jubilation it later turned out that almost all of these were Allied P.O.W.'s, Italian and Greek, being shipped back to Greece.

The Torbeaus were re-organised after their inglorious debut and the new R.A.F. approach was the sensible one of saturating the defences by using swarms of cannon-firing Beaufighters to knock out the warships' flak defences and then to follow up against the thin-skinned vessels with rocket and torpedo to deliver the *coup de grace*. This method was found to work perfectly well in the restricted waters of the North Sea, and by June 1944, the original Strike Wing was joined by a second. With four or five squadrons available for each mission overwhelming firepower was thus deployed as in the case of the attack by the North Coates and Langham Wings against two ships off Schiermonnikoog on 15th. June. The 8,000 ton *Amerskerke* and a 4,000 ton naval auxillary were escorted by seven R. boats and eleven minesweepers. They were hit by 254, 455 and 489 Squadrons as anti-flak strikers, by 254 carrying torpedoes and by 236 armed with the new rocket projectiles.

After thirty-two anti-flak Beaufighters had made their passes the four RP-Beaus fired 32

R.A.F. Coastal Command Beaufighters, bearing D-Day invasion markings, strafe a German armed trawler.

Above: R.A.F. cannon-firing Beaufighters attack a German destroyer escorting a merchant ship to knock out the anti-aircraft defences so that the "Torbeaus" can attack. Below: An armed trawler and a motor vessel on fire after a cannon attack by anti-flak Beaufighters.

An R.A.F. Wellington bomber, equipped with A.S.V. "stickleback" radar, flies over the Adriatic towards Greece.

rockets which scored ten hits on the auxillary and eight on the *Amerskerke.* When the ten Torbeaus followed up, they met no flak and could thus plant two torpedoes into each of the main targets. No aircraft were lost in this assault. This was the greatest of such attacks off Holland but many lesser strikes were made and great carnage was inflicted during the German evacuation of Norway.

The main lesson to be learned from these R.A.F. attacks was not the continued effectiveness of the torpedo, but the overwhelming power of the stand-off rocket. It could not sink large ships, but then Germany had few of these left. The rocket could, however, wreck their upperworks while small vessels could be sunk by rocket alone. This fact marked the demise of the torpedo in the R.A.F. and it was not widely employed post-war.

Italy and Germany

The Sm.79 continued to operate as the main Italian torpedo bomber, though in ever decreasing numbers after the peak of two-hundred at the end of 1942. We have given enough details of the actual ships sunk and damaged by the *Aerosilurante* in these pages to confirm that it was a highly effective unit. However, the *Aerosilurante* were credited with a large number of victories which did not take place. The list of these non-existent successes is reproduced here, together with the true facts.

Ship claimed sunk by SM.79's	Comments and true cause of loss
Eagle (Aircraft carrier)	Sunk by German submarine U.73
Jaguar (Destroyer)	Sunk by German submarine U.652
Legion (Destroyer)	Bombed 3 times by Ju.88's and Ju.87's in dock at Malta, torpedo bombing not possible
Southwall (Destroyer)	No such ship. Possibly the *Southwold* sunk by mines off Malta.
Kujavik II (Destroyer)	No such ship. Possibly Polish *Kujawiak* mined off Malta.
Husky (Destroyer)	No such ship. Possibly the *Hasty* sunk by E. boats in Eastern Med.

This photograph taken in 1943, shows Italian fighter aircraft equipped with experimental torpedoes and bombs.

During the North African landings and the subsequent invasion of Sicily from November 1942 to July 1943, the *Aerosilurante* units co-operated with the German units in frequent attacks on Allied merchant shipping, battle-squadrons and ports. At this time the Axis began to learn the lesson already known by the Allies and the Japanese, i.e. that, although the torpedo bomber was the best weapon for use against shipping, its high success rate could only continue while the anti-aircraft armament on ships was relatively weak or the attacking aircraft were in overwhelming numbers. Once strengthened by the additions of 20-mm, and 40-mm automatic cannon in large numbers the ships were able to make the low approach of the torpedo bomber particularly vulnerable unless swamped by attackers. Aircraft losses when used in penny packets became prohibitive. The Allies and the Japanese learned this lesson early for the Axis and American ships were much better armed than the British in this respect. By 1943, however, the defensive armament of British ships was starting to catch up slowly with the others and torpedo bombers operations thus became equally expensive for all nations.

Although about 120 German and 200 Italian torpedo bombers were on hand on 8th. November 1942, and attacked with great persistence and courage, wastage was very high. The heavy losses of highly trained aircrew suffered throughout November and December were never to be recovered. A principal reason for this was the fuel shortage which started biting on the Axis at this time. The resulting closure of the training schools meant that the supply of new torpedo bomber crews was reduced to a trickle.

A few Focke Wulfe FW.190's were adapted to carry torpedoes at the end of World War II.

An FW.190 armed with a *Hayelkorn* weapon.

Therefore operational efficiency as well as strength was severely hit. At no time during January and February 1943 did the number of German torpedo bombers available exceed fifty or sixty. By March, it was down to five to ten serviceable aircraft. The Italians fared the same. For example, it was in raids against allied shipping at Bougie on the night of the 11th./12th. November, 1942 that Buscaglia was lost leading his unit.

The results gained by Axis torpedo bombers at this time were far from impressive. The number of victories tailed away with the loss of aircrew. The attacks in which Buscaglia died resulted in the sinking of the A.A. ship *Tynwald* and heavy damage to the monitor *Roberts.* The sinking of four large liners the *Cathay, Awatea, Karanja* and *Narkunda* was a greater achievement.

The heavy casualties continued during December with the Axis torpedo bombers being responsible for the sinking of the destroyer *Quentin* off Cape Bon on the 2nd., while the cruiser *Argonaut* was hit by two aerial torpedoes which blew away her bow and stern on the 14th. December. Among the larger liners hit was the *Cameronia* on 22nd. December and *Windsor Castle* on 23rd. February.

A reduction of air attacks was coupled with the drive of the Allied armies along the North African shore until they came to an abrupt halt and back-peddled when they struck the Germans in Tunisia. On March 13th. the new circling torpedoes were dropped in Tripoli harbour and two ships were sunk by them.

The unconventionally designed BV.141 makes a test flight.

Between June and December 1943, the official history of the War at Sea says that some 41 ships of 225,450 tons were sunk by aerial attack in the Mediterranean. Wastage of aircrew continued and by 12th. June there were only twenty Italian torpedo bombers left, together with a few German aircraft operating from bases in South France. The invasion of Sicily followed in July 1943 and the few torpedo bombers available to the Axis succeeded in hitting and damaging the aircraft carrier *Indomitable,* the monitor *Erebus,* three destroyers and three merchant ships.

On the Italian surrender in September 1943, some thirty-four SM.79's joined the Italian Co-Belligerent Air Force although they had little success. The more experienced aircrew joined the Axis *Aviazione della Repubblica Sociale Italiana* and re-equipped with the S.579 as the *Gruppo Buscaglia.* It was led by Captain Faggioni initially. The Allied landings at Salerno gave an opportunity for dusk attacks by torpedo bombers and no less than 155 sorties were made on the night of September 8th./9th., with another 100 the following night. At Anzio in January 1944, torpedo bombers sank the destroyer *Janus* on the 22nd. with heavy loss of life. Captain Faggioni was lost here and replaced by Major Marini.

A Junkers JU.88 carrying two experimental BU.L.10 torpedoes.

Attacks by Ju.88 torpedo bombers from South France took place at night three times during April 1944, but had only partial success. On the 30th. of that month an attack by sixty Ju.88's against convoy UGS.38 off Algiers resulted in the loss of the U.S. destroyer *Landsale* and two 7,000 ton merchantmen with damage to two others. Counter-measures were so effective that, when convoy UGS.40 was attacked by sixty-two Ju.88's on 11th. May, although 91 torpedoes were dropped, no ships were hit and sixteen of the torpedo bombers were destroyed by A.A. defences. On 31st. May, 1944 an attack on convoy KMS.51 by forty Ju.88's sank one ship for the loss of four of the torpedo bombers.

On the night of June 4th./5th. the *Gruppo Buscaglia* made a daring torpedo attack against Gibraltar. The last major torpedo bomber attack of the war in the Mediterranean took place on the night of 1st. August when forty bombers struck convoy UGS.48 off Bougie without scoring any hits. After this, the Ju.88's were withdrawn northward into France.

During the final eighteen month period it was the old Ju.88's that formed the backbone of the Axis torpedo bomber forces, despite the fact that both the Italians and the Germans had sought faster and more modern replacements for them.

Japan and United States

In the Pacific war, the torpedo bomber featured in conjunction with the dive bomber in the great carrier battles of 1943/45. The American advance began with the landing on Guadalcanal in the Solomon Islands on 7th. August, 1942. From then, the Japanese were on the defensive more and more. On the 8th. August, for example, an attack mounted by thirty-two Japanese torpedo bombers met a forwarned defence over the anchorage off the island and seventeen were shot down for the loss of only the single destroyer *Jarvis.* The Japanese 11th. Air Fleet at Rabaul attempted to stem the tide of the U.S. advance at a great cost. Other attacks by small task groups never achieved a positive result and losses grew heavier and heavier.

In the Solomon Islands battle of 23rd. August, 1942 the light carrier *Ryuho* was sunk after attacks by Avengers and Dauntless aircraft from the *Enterprise,* but the Japanese return strike failed to inflict torpedo hits at all. At the Battle of Santa Cruz on 25th. October, the light carrier *Zuiho* was damaged. The *Shokaku* and *Zuikaku* exchanged blows with the *Enterprise* and *Hornet.* The Japanese torpedo bombers led by Lieutenant-Commander Shigeharu Murata and Lieutenant Jiichiro Imajuku put two torpedoes into the *Hornet's* engine room while a third Kate crashed into her forward lift. A further torpedo bomber attack suffered heavily, but again a damaged Kate piled into the destroyer *Smith* destroying her bridge structure. *Hornet* finally sank but the cost to the Japanese was too heavy for this victory to be decisive and Imajuku and Murata were two verteran torpedo bomber leaders who did not come back.

On the 12th. November, 1943 following a night action off Guadalcanal the damaged Japanese battleship *Hiei* was caught by torpedo bombers from the *Enterprise* who hit her twice. She stayed afloat however, and the Avengers returned later to add a further two torpedo hits and the battleship was later scuttled. This same unit from *Enterprise* hit and sank the heavy cruiser *Kinugasa* on 14th. November.

On 29th. January, 1943, Japanese torpedo bombers from Munda hit the heavy cruiser *Chicago* with two torpedoes and next day sank her with four more at the cost of eleven of the twelve attacking aircraft. In August, the Americans took the Ellis Islands and in November, Tarawa. The only outstanding event by the Kate's and Peggy's was a single hit on the carrier *Independence.* The huge American carrier task groups made massive raids against the Marshall Islands and other bases. For example, on 4th. December, a hit was scored on the cruiser *Nagara* at Kwajalein. The Eniwetok Islands fell in February 1944, and Truk, the main Japanese fleet base, was raided with heavy losses to the defenders. The great Marianas battle culminated in the Battle of the Philippine Sea on 19th. June, 1944 when nine Japanese carriers duelled with twelve American. The result was a massacre. 450 aircraft were thrown in by the Japanese and more than 300 were destroyed. U.S. losses were much less and the U.S. torpedo bombers in return sank the carrier *Hiyo* and damaged several other ships.

When the Americans landed in the Philippines, the Battle of Leyte Gulf erupted and U.S. torpedo bombers were heavily engaged. The giant battleship *Musashi* was hit by no less than twenty-six torpedoes from the swarming Avengers before she sank while on the same day, 24th. October, 1944, they hit the cruiser *Myoko.* On the 25th., the Avengers torpedoed the cruiser *Tama,* the carrier *Chitose* and the destroyer *Akitsuki.* Next, the carrier *Chiyoda* went

Above: A BU.L.10 torpedo being launched from a Heinkel He.117 bomber.

down. Further south in this wide ranging battle, the biggest sea fight of all time, torpedo bombers help sink the cruiser *Kumano.*

Again in the north, the carriers *Zuikaku* and *Zuiho* were sunk. The few Japanese torpedo bombers that managed to take part were overwhelmed by the defending fighters and a flak barrage over the American fleet that was larger than that for the entire British Isles. They were wiped out without result, which convinced the Japanese of the futility of further conventional attacks and led to the adoption of *Kamikaze* tactics.

The American fleet however still had ample targets for their Avengers and during the closing months of the war, the mighty battleship *Yamato* was put down with seven or more torpedoes. The rest of the Japanese fleet was destroyed at anchor due to lack of fuel. Without any doubt it was the combination of torpedo bombers and dive bombers which won the Pacific War at sea. Land based torpedo bombing had never been much featured in the U.S. Navy in contrast to the Japanese strength there. One exception was the Navy version of the Mitchell, the North American PBJ.10 Patrol Bomber. It could carry a standard navy torpedo externally and was used in the South West Pacific by Marine flyers.

1945 and after

Orthodox torpedo bomber development continued in the closing stages of the war in both the Royal and the United States Navy despite the scarcity of suitable targets. In Britain the final results were the Blackburn Firebrand and the Fairey Spearfish. The Firebrand design was begun in 1940 but was not delivered to squadron service until 1945; too late for wartime operations. It was a splendid aircraft, a single-seater monoplane, powered by a 2,500 horse power Bristol Centaurus IX engine which gave it a maximum speed of 350 m.p.h. with a range of 740 miles. Span was 51 feet 3½ inches, length was 38 feet 11 inches and height 14 feet 11 inches. It could carry a 1,850 pound torpedo, externally. It served afloat with 827 squadron aboard *Eagle* in 1952/53. The Fairey Spearfish was a great improvement over the Barracuda but again too late. Powered by a 2,320 horse power Bristol Centaurus engine it had a maximum speed of only 292 m.p.h. but a range of 1,036 miles and could carry its torpedo internally for the first time in a Royal Navy torpedo bomber. It never saw production.

The U.S. Navy was similarly placed with the Consolidated TBY.2 Seawolf torpedo bomber. Originally designed by Vought some 140 were built in 1945 too late for war service.

The Germans also had hopes of making the torpedo bomber a viable proposition again by

Left: A BU.L.10 torpedo. Above: Gannet anti-submarine aircraft of 825 Squadron from H.M.S. *Eagle* flying into Malta where they are to be based ashore. February 1958.

a combination of new aircraft and 'stand off' torpedoes to overcome the heavy flak problem. Despite extensive trials however it was once more a case of too late. As Hitler himself recorded, he had been advised against developing the torpedo bomber pre-war, now he was asked for it when there was little hope of achieving production. With the abandonment of the South France bases in 1944 the new bombers and new weapons were useless.

Post-War, the two surviving Naval powers continued to develop the orthodox carrier-borne torpedo bomber. In Britain the Westland Wyvern and finally the Fairey Gannet finished the story. The Wyvern was seven years in production. A single-seater monoplane, it was powered by a 4,100 horse power Armstrong-Siddeley Python A.S.P.3 with a speed of 383 m.p.h. and a range of 904 miles. It first entered service in May 1953 with 813 squadron and later served aboard *Eagle* and *Albion* including ground attack service during the Suez operation in November, 1956. The Gannet was a combined strike and search aircraft. A three seater with a 2,950 horse power Armstrong-Siddeley Double Mamba engine. It could carry two homing torpedoes in its internal bomb bay. It went into service in 1955 and was the last operational torpedo bomber of the Fleet Air Arm.

The U.S. Navy developed the Douglas Skyraider, one of the most long-serving aircraft of all time, as a torpedo bomber originally and used it in this role for the last time during the Korean War. On 4th. May, 1954 the Hawchon Dam was demolished by Skyraiders using aerial torpedoes when ordinary bombing failed. The dam was blown up to break up Communist grouping in preparation for the Spring offensive.

It was the end of the torpedo bomber story.

Above: The Fairey Firebrand was developed too late to see service in World War II. Below: The Fairey Spearfish was the first British torpedo bomber to carry its missile internally.